INVESTORS ᴵᴺ PEOPLE MAINTAINED

Peter Taylor
Bob Thackwray

INVESTORS IN PEOPLE

MAINTAINED

KOGAN
PAGE

First published 1999

Kogan Page Limited
120 Pentonville Road
London
N1 9JN
UK

Stylus Publishing Inc.
22883 Quicksilver Drive
Sterling
VA 20166-2012
USA

For further information regarding Investors in People, please contact your local Training and Enterprise Council (TEC) in England and Wales, Local Enterprise Company (LEC) in Scotland or the Training and Employment Agency in Northern Ireland. Alternatively write to Investors in People UK, 7–10 Chandos Street, London W1M 9DE.

British Library Cataloguing in Publication Data

A CIP record for this book is available from the British Library.

ISBN 0 7494 2920 8

Typeset by JS Typesetting, Wellingborough, Northants
Printed and bound by Clays Ltd, St Ives plc

Contents

Appendices

References   177

Index   179

Acknowledgements

The authors gratefully acknowledge the contributions made by a large number of organizations and individuals, especially: Duncan Collins, The Hambledon Group; Eamonn Harris, John Marincowicz and Colin Price, Queen Elizabeth's Boys School; Ian Luxford, Investors in People UK; Gillian Malkin, HR Director Barnsley; Michael Parkinson OBE, Chairman, Airedale; Jonathon Simnett, Director, Brodeur A Plus; Ruth Spellman, Chief Executive, Investors in People UK; Peter Tingley, Bidwells; Heinz Volland, General Manager Renaissance London Heathrow Hotel; Sue Webb, National Assessor with Investors in People UK; David Williams, University of Sunderland; David Wormald, MD Raflatac Limited.

Introduction

The Investors in People Standard is now widely recognized as the framework that helps organizations develop through the development of their people.

By May 1999, 14,478 organizations had been recognized as an Investor in People – meeting the National Standard for effective investment in people. By the same date another 21,424 organizations had made the commitment to become an Investor in People, involving a total of around 8 million people or 34 per cent of the workforce. Of those recognized over 2,800 were re-recognitions.

This book is designed to be of use and interest to a wide variety of organizations and individuals, and to students and trainers alike. It examines a range of issues that organizations have faced following initial recognition. It begins, in essence, where our previous book *Investors in People Explained* ended. If you or your organization want to know more about the Standard, or if you are at any stage in the process, *Investors in People Explained* will provide some answers and, without a doubt pose a few more questions!

The book is aimed primarily at organizations that have demonstrated that they have met the Investors in People Standard and are looking to gain further organizational or business benefits by continuing to meet the Standard. The intention is that it should offer practical suggestions and advice on the major issues and potential pitfalls.

The book has been designed in three parts. Part One looks at those major issues faced by organizations following their first recognition. It starts by examining the process, then looks at ways of embedding the culture of continuous improvement and what happens when, almost inevitably at some stage, momentum is lost.

Part Two describes the experiences of organizations that have been reassessed and the benefits they gained from the process. In Part Three we offer a variety of instruments, techniques and strategies that can be used to support the processes of embedding and continuous improvement. In response to reader demand and the feedback on areas of interest and concern nationally with regard to Investors in People, there is a particular focus on evaluation.

As with *Investors in People Explained* it is intended as a working document. It can be read from beginning to end or particular sections can be 'dipped into'. All sections and chapters can therefore be read independently of the rest: they are 'stand alone' accounts of particular elements of the post-recognition process.

Part One: Maintaining and Retaining Recognition

Chapter 1 reviews the type of issues that emerge from the first assessment that should be considered when planning how to maintain recognition. We look at the key issue of embedding the changed culture; how Investors in People can become part of the way organizations operate and therefore minimize the work involved in preparing for reassessment.

Chapter 2 examines the reassessment process now known as the post-recognition review process. It covers the development of the process describing how the lessons learnt from the first reassessments were heeded and built in to the new model. We examine the concept of continuous improvement in relation to Investors in People. It also examines what 'continued commitment' means.

In Chapter 3 we examine the issue of continuous improvement and how organizations have addressed the feedback issues identified by assessors following the first assessment. Chapter 4 looks at issues around, for what many people think are the difficult areas of planning and evaluation. In Chapter 5 the authors revisit the role of line managers and the issues around their further development.

Chapter 6 looks at the issues faced by large and multi-sited organizations as they strive to achieve maintained recognition and consider some of the issues for recognition for the organization as a whole. Chapter 7 re-examines the Investors in People indicators and highlights where there may be a different emphasis at the post-recognition review stage. Finally in this section, Chapter 8 looks at sources of help.

Part Two: The Experiences

What was it like for some of those organizations that have already gone through the reassessment process? This part of the book includes a range of case studies that reveal salient elements of the highs and lows of the initial 'journey' and then focuses on what was done to continue to meet the Standard. It looks at what they gained from the initial experience and why they wanted to continue to be recognized as an Investor in People. The organizations selected were chosen for reasons of size, type and nature of activity, and the variety of experience they collectively offered.

Two of the organizations (Brodeur A Plus and the Renaissance Hotel) were included in the first and second editions of *Investors in People Explained*. It was not appropriate to include all the earlier case studies as some have merged or were about to change as this book was being prepared. One of the case studies, Fujitsu Microelectronics Durham Ltd, closed due to the market for microchips changing. However, during the last few months Fujitsu continued to demonstrate its commitment to its workforce by ensuring that those undergoing training completed it to enable them to compete for new jobs.

The case studies featured in this book are:

I.   Airedale Springs;
II.   Barnsley Community and Priority NHS Trust;
III.   Bidwells;
IV.   Brodeur A Plus;
V.   Queen Elizabeth's Boys School;
VI.   Raflatac Limited;
VII.   Renaissance London Heathrow Hotel;
VIII. University of Sunderland.

Part Three: Some Strategies and Tools

This section offers advice and support for individuals and their organizations as they continue to maintain and develop their

Investors in People status. It begins with a look at evaluation, the element of the Standard that normally concerns organizations the most. An examination of the Donald Kirkpatrick four-level model of evaluation is followed by a look at some other evaluation tools, techniques and instruments. As many indicators and related evidence require information on attitude, behaviour and effectiveness, we then offer an examination of these key areas. Ways of finding out 'how well we are doing' are examined and the section concludes with a look at how to develop a responsive evaluation strategy.

Finally, there are two appendices. The first one gives the full National Standard and the 23 indicators, and the second is an example of a pre- and post-debriefing pro forma.

CHAPTER 1

Maintaining the Momentum

This opening chapter examines the events and reactions immediately following initial recognition as an Investor in People. It will be of potential interest and value to most readers as it sets the scene for the subsequent chapters by outlining typical issues included in the feedback given to the organization by the assessor. It gives an overview of how the Training and Enterprise Council (TEC) will seek to maintain contact during the period between recognition and the date when reassessment is due. Finally it explores the developing of an action plan to take them forward to the first reassessment.

Recovering from the first recognition!

Once the celebrations are complete, the reaction of most organizations after being recognized as an Investor in People is to do one of two things: relax and assume that the processes and systems will continue to work; or recognize that maintaining and retaining recognition is not necessarily any easier than gaining it in the first place. There is an understandable level of excitement and enthusiasm generated while undertaking the 'journey' and achieving recognition. Typically this soon passes and things begin to 'plateau'.

In some organizations systems may well be embedded and will continue to operate. For many they won't, at least not without continued effort. Our experience is that a significant number of organizations have had to introduce a range of new processes and systems in order to attain Investors in People status. Even when systems appear embedded they may atrophy, if care is not taken to review and modify them to keep them fresh and motivate people (especially line managers) to continue to use them and, importantly, to continue to recognize the value of continuing to use them. It is at this point that the additional indicator (4.5) may help. The indicator states that: 'Action takes place to implement improvements to training and development identified as a result of evaluation.' Continuous evaluation to review and improve processes can lead to them being kept fresh.

As we described in our book *Managing For Investors in People*, systems rely on managers at all levels to operate them – and to 'own' them. Many organizations note that rarely, if ever, are all managers 'fully on board'. They may have been willing to operate the systems in order to help the organization satisfy its goal of recognition but once it has been achieved some may revert to their old ways. It's what we call 'public consensus and private disruption'. Some may intend to keep operating the systems but for one reason or another they don't. The systems may be too complex or bureaucratic and therefore a busy manager may find other, more important things to do. Some organizations may have driven sceptical or task-focused managers to use the systems. For these people Investors in People will have been viewed, inevitably, as an additional chore.

In some organizations, even though they may have satisfied an assessor, meaningful benefits from Investors in People for managers may take some time to emerge. If the organizations fail to encourage their more sceptical or less committed managers to keep using the systems these benefits may never emerge.

The Brodeur A Plus case study (Case Study IV) is an illustration of the above. Following their first assessment, because of other priorities, they had lost the focus on recording and evaluating the personal development that had taken place. The process of taking stock while preparing for reassessment alerted them to this fact and the lesson was built in for subsequent reassessments.

The immediate post-recognition phase is therefore very important. The actions needed to continue to demonstrate that the Investors in People Standard is met should be planned carefully. They should build on the action taken prior to assessment and be designed to embed the processes into the organizational culture. They should take account of any lessons learnt during the assessment and also the feedback from the assessor at the end of it.

Post-assessment feedback to organization

The first significant lessons learnt from the early assessments highlighted the importance and 'added value' of offering feedback to organizations, following the decision by the recognition panel to recognize an organization. This has been a developmental feature of the national Standard itself. Recent market research by Investors in People UK shows that the feedback meeting has grown in importance and is now seen by employers, with the site visit, as the most valuable element of the process. Hence the development of the Standard has incorporated the feedback as the key agenda-setting device for continuous improvement and subsequent assessments.

One of the benefits of an experienced, external assessor examining the processes and systems within an organization is that they invariably discover that although processes and systems may be working effectively, they can always be improved. This was further encouraged by recognition panels who were increasingly very suspicious of assessors' reports of organizations that appeared 'too good'. Assessors were and continue to be encouraged to present a picture that is realistic and includes issues that, although meeting the requirements of the Standard, could be improved. Recognition panels themselves also offer assessors a range of items that they would like fed back to organizations. (The role of the panel is, as noted elsewhere, moving towards a more developmental one, although they will still confirm first recognitions.)

While stressing the importance of feedback it is also worth pointing out that the focus is on issues emerging through the assessment process. Organizations should therefore not, of course, expect a full consultancy report but they should get a number of practical ideas for further improvement that in the main have emanated from the staff themselves and been refined and pulled together by the assessor. The assessor must necessarily be careful when offering feedback as the feedback should not stray into advice. If it does it will disqualify the assessor from carrying out the reassessment as the guidelines quite clearly state that an assessor should not assess their own advice. The assessor is therefore confined to feeding back what the issues may be, why they should be considered but not how to address them. Normally the feedback is given by the assessor with an advisor from the TEC present. Following feedback on the 'what' and the 'why' the assessor will then withdraw and the TEC advisor will discuss with the representative of the organization the 'how', ie how these issues can be taken forward and whether the TEC can offer any further support. In the spirit of *kaizen* (the search for a better way), most organizations welcome this feedback.

Typical issues discussed during feedback

It is frequently stated that organizations do not have to be perfect to meet the Investors in People Standard. They merely need to demonstrate that they meet the requirements of the indicators so inevitably there will be areas of strength and some which require further development. Although many organizations often realize themselves that some systems which are in place could be much more effective through further improvement, an external assessor may spot additional areas for development. These emerge during the course of an assessment as experienced assessors will recognize where systems and processes could be further developed but in addition employees who are interviewed use the opportunity to make suggestions.

Experience has shown that there are a number of common issues that involve embedding the processes and developing the culture. They can be grouped as follows:

- adding clarity through existing processes, eg through communications structures;
- planning and evaluation issues;
- consolidation of processes to ensure cohesion;
- further development of managers;
- issues that have been already recognized by organizations and included in future plans.

An analysis of these headings reveals the following issues most often arising.

Adding clarity

- developing further the understanding of issues, plans, etc;
- reviewing effectiveness of communications periodically to avoid complacency appearing;
- ensuring 'all' employees continue to be included, ie support staff, non-directs (staff not directly employed by the organization), etc;
- increasing the involvement of people;
- giving a higher profile to *development* as opposed to training;
- further definition of roles and responsibilities, eg managing training and development;
- defining management 'effectiveness';
- expanding the 'buzz' from the shop floor to include the office areas.

Planning and evaluation issues

- examining the quality of objectives at individual, team and organizational levels;
- ensuring they are specific, measurable, achievable, realistic and timebound (SMART), or in many cases SMARTer;
- increasing clarity about *planned* benefits especially at the organizational level;
- improving planning, and building in more structure to the development process as the focus shifts from formal training courses to development and learning on the job – the use of Personal Development Plans is often a suggestion to aid this process;
- using training matrices to plan and monitor training and development activity at team levels;
- strengthening the links between business/organizational needs and training and development to reduce wastage, ie training that is not used;
- improving the quantification of benefits all round;
- increasing recognition of the benefits of the training and development activities.

Consolidation and cohesion

- reviewing immature planning processes to make them slicker and simpler to administer;
- reviewing complex and over-elaborate systems;
- identifying where processes and systems overlap and duplicate activity;
- integrating what may appear as 'Investors in People processes' into the existing business or organizational processes;
- reducing the dependency on auditing or policing systems to ensure compliance by ensuring systems become part of the organizational culture.

Further development of managers

- refreshing and updating management skills;
- examining the appropriateness of competences, the management NVQs, etc to ensure managers are clear what is expected of them;
- where organizations have empowered their staff, ensuring that managers do not abdicate their responsibilities altogether;
- in some organizations encouraging managers to be more pro-active in inviting their people to identify and take up training and development opportunities.

As indicated earlier, many organizations may already have some of these and other issues, such as expanding the use of NVQs and developing competence frameworks, included in their plans.

The need for a portfolio

Although the use of portfolios of evidence is now being questioned, at the time of writing many organizations are still preparing portfolios for their first assessment and some for their first reassessment. (There has never been a requirement for a portfolio. This has been further re-emphasized by Investors in People UK in 1999. The only written requirements are: the strategic plan, the staff training and development policy, and a statement on resources for training and development.) Over the years portfolios have become, in the main, much more streamlined and better presented but research has shown that they are time-consuming to prepare and they tend to reinforce an unnecessary bureaucracy. Indeed, they are wholly inappropriate for some organizations. The time that is spent putting them together clearly adds to the cost of assessment.

Initially it was felt the portfolio would be a universally useful document, particularly for smaller organizations. The expectation was that the portfolio, the production of which may have been the first time an organization had collated material, would evolve into their training and development manual. Some organizations were therefore encouraged to maintain and update a portfolio as a useful exercise following recognition. However, for other organizations it was agreed that this might not be a useful task. It was left, therefore, to each organization to decide what was best for them. It was often recommended that the portfolio was kept intact as it might be useful for the assessor at the reassessment stage but in reality assessors rarely look at them at the reassessment stage. With the changes to the reassessment process, outlined later in this book (Chapter 2), many organizations now coming forward for reassessment are unlikely to produce portfolios.

The role of the TEC and LEC following recognition

The level of support following recognition, either financial or in other ways, varies from one Training and Enterprise Council (TEC) or Local Enterprise Council (LEC) to another. Following the early assessments it is now recognized that TEC/LECs probably did not maintain sufficient structured contact during the period up to reassessment. This has improved but, with the focus still on encouraging more organizations to commit, TEC/LEC resources are clearly stretched.

Following the feedback meeting, if asked, the TEC/LEC advisor may work with the company to develop an action plan to work towards reassessment. There may be further support for management development or NVQs but this needs to be taken up with the TEC/LEC advisor.

Many TEC/LECs have encouraged organizations that have been recognized to continue networking to support one another following recognition and frequently provide opportunities to do so. Others invite recognized organizations to make presentations at events and encourage involvement in recognition panels. All these offer opportunities to continue to learn and develop ideas that encourage different approaches to build on the first stages of the journey to excellence through Investors in People. The TEC/LEC will remind you when your reassessment is due and advise you on how to present your case.

To plan or not to plan

As already indicated, planning the actions following recognition is important. Some TECs encourage the development of a post-recognition action plan while others are ambivalent about them. The authors feel that as part of the consolidation process care should be taken to ensure that any Investors in People processes are not seen as separate issues but are integrated into the normal organizational processes. (As Juran puts it: 'fitness for purpose'.) It is important to emphasize that Investors in People does not lay down requirements as such. In the past some people misguidedly have over-focused on paper-based bureaucratic appraisal systems. (There is no requirement for a formal written appraisal scheme.) These can often be inappropriate for some types of smaller organizations and some categories of employee in larger ones. The planning of any action to be taken as a result of feedback following recognition should therefore be included in the normal planning process.

Issues such as reviewing communication, training and development and other processes should be carried out in a way that is relevant to the needs and objectives of the organization. The aims, values and objectives of the organization should influence the way in which managers are developed. Increasing involvement of people can be carried out by involving them in the planning process (see Chapter 4).

Changes in business direction, product range, technology, etc present opportunities to use the Investors framework to plan, communicate the plans, identify and act upon any training or development needed and check the effectiveness of the action. By doing this continually organizations should be able to demonstrate they are continuing to meet the Standard.

Remember . . . *simplicity, practicality and relevance are the keys. Cohesion through integration and consolidation is the rule.*

Summary

This first chapter is the scene setter for the rest of the book. Issues raised will be explored further in subsequent chapters. We have examined the importance of the feedback at the end of the first and subsequent assessments and the continuing role of the TEC/LEC. Attention has been drawn to the typical issues that emerge from assessments and that they should be included in the normal planning processes of the organization. Finally we have stressed the need for integration and consolidation of processes in order to keep them fresh and actively used by managers.

CHAPTER 2

The Reassessment Process (The Post-recognition Review Process)

This chapter examines the process previously referred to as reassessment and will again be of value to all readers. For those interested in the history of the process, it covers how it has developed, who was involved, the rationale behind decisions and the current position. For recognized organizations, it describes what options they have for review to enable them to make appropriate plans for the first and subsequent review.

The background to the development of the process

The debates over reassessment: why three years?

When Investors in People was first developed, the idea was that recognition could last for a maximum of three years and it would be up to TEC/LECs to decide if they wanted to reassess within that period. At that time most TEC/LECs indicated they were likely to wait the full three-year period before reassessing. To maintain national consistency it was therefore decided that there would be no optional time frame and all recognitions should last for three years.

However, following the first recognitions many organizations asked the question: 'Why wait as long as three years?' Consideration of a number of factors gave rise to the view that at that time three years was thought to be an appropriate period of time. These can be summarized as follows:

- Investors in People concerns strategic planning. It is possible that some organizations may not be able to demonstrate some of the significant improvements and benefits in less than that period.
- There was a commonly held view which felt that organizations would understandably question the logic of having an assessment every year in terms of cost and added value.
- TECs would not be able to cope with the resource implications of reassessing every year.

The continuing development and refinement of the reassessment process

In 1993 the Board of Investors in People UK laid down the following, overriding principle that once the organization had proved that they had met the Standard, the purpose of the reassessment was to prove that they had maintained it. The thinking behind this was that:

- the credibility of the Standard should be maintained;
- there is a need to avoid unnecessary bureaucracy and cost;
- the reassessment should be business-plan driven;
- it should focus on changes;
- it should be completed within the third anniversary of the original assessment.

The Board stated that the process should comprise:

- an examination of the accumulated evidence, original portfolio and the assessor report;

- interviews with a small sample of employees to confirm that the original and any new arrangements are in place and working effectively;
- a report by the assessor to a recognition panel;
- a decision by the panel.

The reassessment project

After the first reassessments, because there was some dissatisfaction with the process, the debate about the reassessment process was rekindled. A project involving 350 organizations was commissioned in 1995 to examine the issues around reassessment. During the project, the reassessment process was thoroughly re-examined. The main concerns that emerged from the organizations were:

- the cost of reassessment;
- the perceived added value at reassessment;
- bureaucracy;
- inflexibility of timing.

The project also identified that the things that clients valued from assessments (and reassessments) were:

- the assessors' site visit;
- the report;
- immediate feedback and recommendations for continuous improvement;
- regular contact with the TEC;
- that Investors in People is an external benchmark:
- continuity of process and recognition.

A new model was developed for reassessment which aimed to:

- provide an attractive alternative option for reassessment;
- be of more use as business development tool;
- reduce the perceived bureaucracy and cost;
- maintain the rigour and integrity of the Standard.

The emerging reassessment models

Two options emerged from the pilot project. The first was a new model that involved organizations, once they were recognized, drawing up an agreement with the assessment unit which involved a 'service agreement' for maintenance of the Standard. This model, introduced in June 1998, offered a series of approximately annual (12–15 months) visits by an assessor, and agreed development actions against the Standard on an ongoing basis with a smaller and lower-cost three-year review. The second option, for those who want it, is the status quo; in other words a portfolio of evidence followed by site visits. From June 1998 recognized organizations were invited to choose which model they wanted to opt for. There was an element of retrospection in that organizations recognized after June 1997 were also invited to choose which model they wanted to opt for. Those recognized prior to that date will be reassessed using the original model after which it is intended that they will then be invited to choose from the two models for future reassessments.

However, there was still an element of dissatisfaction with the restrictive nature of the 12–15-month period so Investors in People UK decided that the constraint of 12–15 months would be removed. From July 1999 there will be one model through which organizations will be allowed to choose when they wish to be reassessed provided that it takes place *at least once every three years*.

The new model will be known as a review (full title: post-recognition review – see Figure 2.1) rather than a reassessment. The following has been adapted from the guidelines issued to the Investors delivery network in June 1999.

Post-recognition reviews

What is the purpose of the post-recognition review?

Post-recognition review enables the organization to demonstrate whether, on an ongoing basis, it continues to meet the Standard. While organizations do not have to meet the Standard at a higher level the next time around, there should be a focus on change and how the principles of the Standard are contributing to improvements and encouraging continuous development within the organization.

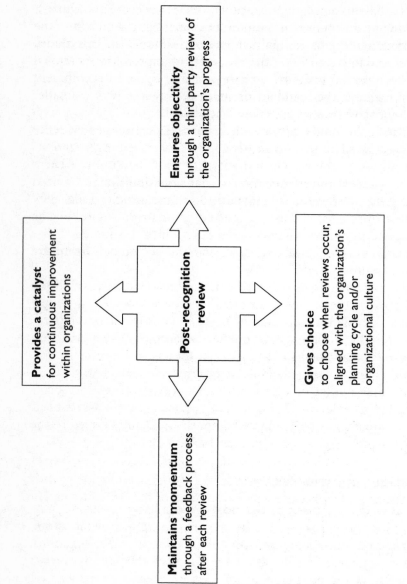

Post-recognition review

Provides a catalyst for continuous improvement within organizations

Ensures objectivity through a third party review of the organization's progress

Gives choice to choose when reviews occur, aligned with the organization's planning cycle and/or organizational culture

Maintains momentum through a feedback process after each review

Figure 2.1 *The post-recognition model (Source: Investors in People UK)*

What are the options for post-recognition reviews?

Once an organization has been recognized as an Investor in People, it will need to decide how frequently it wishes to be reviewed against the Standard. There is no minimum or pre-set rule on the time period between post-recognition reviews, although the maximum period between recognition and post-recognition review (or between post-recognition reviews) is three years. It is the organization's decision, through discussion with its assessor/adviser team, to choose when the next review will take place.

This choice could be covered by a service-level agreement if the client wishes. This should clearly specify:

- the assessor and the organization's responsibilities;
- the review process, including any documentation requirements and timescales;
- what will happen following the review visit;
- the process for changing the agreed time period between post-recognition reviews;
- the expected time involved and the associated costs of the review.

What should be considered when deciding on the time interval between post-recognition reviews?

Organizations have the choice in deciding how they continue to meet the Investors in People Standard. They may adopt an approach of either regular three-year reviews (the maximum time limit between reviews), or they may adopt a more frequent or irregular approach.

Each approach to review is equally rigorous and covers the whole Standard. There is no 'right' option. Each organization, along with the assessor/adviser team, will need to look at the key issues facing the organization and determine which option best fits their needs. Table 2.1 may help in determining which option best suits certain organizations.

How will the review be conducted?

There are no definitive rules on how a post-recognition review should be conducted at specific time periods. The assessor will

Table 2.1 *Rationale for review option*

Factor	Frequent reviews (eg 12 months apart)	Less frequent reviews (up to 3 years)
1. Is the organization's environment subject to frequent or rapid change?	✓	✗
2. Does the organization display a high rate of change in its internal operations?	✓	✗
3. Does the organization undertake its own self-assessment or review against the Standard? If so, does this provide adequate confidence to the organization in the ongoing maintenance of the Standard, and feed into its continuous improvement planning?	✗	✓
4. Would the organization value a regular external and independent benchmarking of itself against the Investors in People Standard?	✓	✗
5. Does the organization wish to spread the costs associated with continuing to meet the Standard?	✓	✗
6. Does the organization find the review of itself by other external organizations intrusive or disruptive to the culture of the organization?	✗	✓
7. Is the organization working with any other standard or approach, which involves regular review (eg annual), that could be integrated with the Investors in People review?	✓	✗
8. Other factors, which the assessor/ advisor team might identify, will impact upon the post-recognition review approach	?	?

Note: Where neither extreme is representative of the organization, perhaps it is best to opt for a review period that sits at a point between the extremes. It may well be the case that opportunity and client workload will determine the time of review as much as any of the above.
Source: Investors in People UK

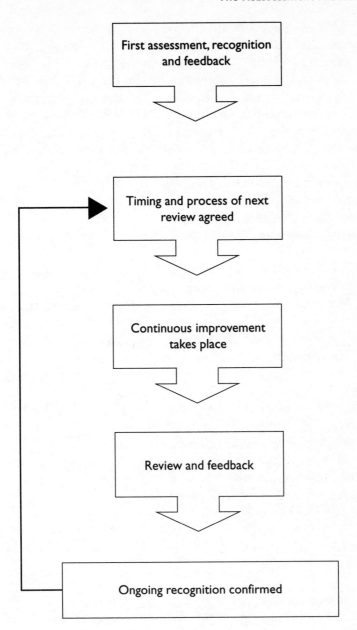

Figure 2.2 *Overview of the post-recognition review process (Source: Investors in People UK)*

agree with the most appropriate method and the amount of assessor time that is required.

The Investors in People UK Guidelines suggest that 'the more frequent approach will require less time than for a full three-year review, but should provide the same degree of coverage over a series of visits as that achieved in one full-scale review every three years'. The experience of the 12–15-month model gives an outline of how this new model is likely to work in practice. First the rules:

- no requirement for a portfolio;
- no recognition panel;
- an immediate decision by the assessor;
- immediate feedback.

The focus of the new model will be on 'audit trailing' or tracking the use of the Investors framework in relation to how the organization has managed changes. Prior to the reassessment the organization will be asked to provide information on changes since their last assessment or review. Where appropriate this can be done on site. The likely changes will include:

- changes in ownership;
- growth/decline;
- structure;
- senior management or key personnel;
- introduction of other quality or business development tools;
- changes to markets/new products;
- introduction of IT/new legislation;
- changes to key processes.

In addition to the above information the organization will be expected to provide:

- current organization charts;
- information about employees in a format similar to the original assessment;
- written evidence of planning process, ie business or operational plan, training and development plans, and the resources required to deliver the training or development.

Where the organization agrees, the same assessor will continue to carry out the reviews following an initial assessment. There was an intention that after three assessments another assessor would then be appointed for subsequent reviews, but this rule has now been rescinded.

Assessors review the above documentation, identifying business objectives and linked training and development. They use the change information to track the process of managing the change to identify how 'clusters' or trails of indicators were met. The feedback issues in the previous assessment report are also considered when planning how the review will be carried out.

An example of a 'trail' may involve how a new product was planned and introduced. Assessors will review how people were informed about it, and how the training needs of the appropriate people were identified and actioned in order to produce it. Finally the training will be evaluated to identify whether it helped people to learn and apply the new skills and if the training needed to be improved for future trainees. The cluster of indicators this time is likely to be as shown in Table 2.2.

Table 2.2 *Indicators of training (see Appendix 1)*

1.3	2.1	2.2	2.3	2.6	3.1	3.3	3.6	4.1	4.2	4.3	4.5
✓	✓	✓	✓	✓	✓	✓	✓	✓	✓	✓	✓

Other 'trails' may involve:

- how new people were inducted;
- how they were briefed about the aims and purpose of the organization;
- the contribution they will be expected to make;
- how their training needs were identified, actioned and evaluated.

The process should reinforce how the organization is committed to their training and development, the opportunities available and could describe how access to qualifications may be available. The

Table 2.3 *Indicators of induction process (see Appendix 1)*

1.1	1.2	1.3	2.3	2.6	2.7	3.1	3.3	3.4	3.5	3.6	4.1/2
✓	✓	✓	✓	✓	✓	✓	✓	✓	✓	✓	✓

cluster of indicators covered by this type of process is likely to be as shown in Table 2.3.

At the same time the assessor will be ensuring that all other indicators are met. The review will also identify areas of strength and areas for future development. Statistics are not available concerning the numbers opting for the new model so far but we feel they are a significant proportion. At the time of writing, just 12 months since the reassessment project was completed, however, the early feedback, based on the 12–15-month review, which is basically the same as the new model, has been favourable:

- Organizations seem to like the less formal approach and the fact that they do not need a portfolio.
- As the review is linked to business processes rather than indicator-driven it appears more relevant.
- They get an immediate decision.
- They also get feedback on how effective the Investors process has been in helping them manage any changes that may have occurred since the last assessment.
- Assessors like it as the process is simpler and the reporting process less time-consuming
- They also like seeing how the organization has developed since the previous assessment.

Summary

This chapter has reviewed the development of the reassessment process, through the early days of reassessment, pilot projects, etc. It has described the emergence of a new post-recognition review model, which will operate from 1 July 1999.

CHAPTER 3

Continuing to Improve

This chapter examines how organizations have addressed some of the feedback issues identified by assessors following the first assessment. It starts by examining the processes that may need evaluating and possible streamlining post-recognition. It looks at the indicator that relates to the concept of continuous improvement (indicator 4.5 – introduced following the 1995/96 review of the Standard and often referred to as the 'new' indicator). It then goes on to examine communications processes and those which identify and meet the training and development needs of individuals and teams.

The feedback issues following the first assessment that are dealt with in this chapter are:

Adding clarity

- developing further the understanding of issues, plans, etc;
- reviewing effectiveness of communications periodically to avoid complacency appearing;
- ensuring 'all' employees continue to be included i.e. support staff, non-directs, etc;
- increasing the involvement of people;
- defining management 'effectiveness';
- expanding the 'buzz' from the shop floor to include the office areas.

Consolidation and cohesion

- reviewing immature planning processes to make them slicker and simple to administer;
- reviewing complex and over elaborate systems;
- identifying where processes and systems overlap and duplicate activity.

Reviewing the systems

The experience that has been gained during the eight years since the first assessments took place demonstrates that the vast majority of organizations have found it necessary to take some action in order to meet the requirements of the Investors in People Standard. For many organizations this has included developing one or more of the following:

- communications processes, such as team briefing, to ensure people understand what the organizations are trying to achieve and how they contribute to team and organizational objectives;
- development review systems (or, in some cases, appraisal systems) which identify training and development needs;
- pro formas and other processes which encourage managers and employees to manage the training and development process, eg carry out pre-event briefings and post-event debriefings, monitor the application of training (see Appendix 2);
- minuting meetings to demonstrate that training and development does feature on the agenda *and* in the discussion during meetings at the various levels of the organization;
- the development of steering groups or focus groups to oversee the development of Investors and address issues that require action;
- the development of a range of evaluative strategies that look beyond the initial response (the 'happy sheet') and focus on applying the learning and the impact on the business.

Quite often these developments have led to a number of processes which overlap and cause duplication. Some systems may have been designed to offer a 'belt and braces' approach to ensure reluctant managers address all the issues that can be addressed and therefore may be more complex than perhaps they need to be. Some organizations may have empowered staff or have taken the view that ownership of systems is important and therefore allowed people or teams to develop their own processes. This can be the case particularly in large and/or multi-site organizations, which are not too centrally driven, and many wheels may well have been reinvented.

The period following recognition is a time to take stock of the systems and identify where some of the above complexity, overlap or duplication exists. For many organizations this is where the process of demonstrating continuous improvement begins.

Continuous improvement

One of the changes that was introduced when the Investors in People indicators were revised in 1996 was to introduce a new indicator: 'Action takes place to implement improvements to training and development identified as a result of evaluation' (4.5). A number of people argued that this indicator was unnecessary as it was implicit in the Standard but its explicit inclusion ensured that organizations could not play lip-service to the concept.

The concept of continuous improvement, as we now know it, appeared in Britain when organizations started to examine the concept of total quality and this led to taking a look at how Japanese companies managed their businesses. Many of these used the approach known as *kaizen*, the search for a better way. The introduction of this new indicator asked organizations to use the kaizen approach to improve the processes used to manage people and their training and development.

An interesting point to note is that this indicator has been placed among the evaluation indicators. The rationale for this is simple. Clearly it is the evaluation processes that will identify where training and development activity needs improving. Similarly evaluation of the processes and systems will identify where they can be developed and improved.

With the focus on continuous improvement it is easy to overlook 'maintenance objectives', continuing to keep a focus on what people already do well and tell them so, as well as looking at continuous improvement. Good evidence for 4.5 could be the recognition following an evaluation that skills in some areas are above and beyond the call of duty and that maintenance objectives together with positive feedback were introduced/enhanced.

The use of improvement groups

Organizations that have introduced aspects of total quality management often introduced it through the use of 'improvement groups',[1] usually cross-functional and often with people from different levels within the organization. However, not all organizations used this approach and those that did may not have used it to its full potential. Maintaining the Investors Standard provides an opportunity to involve people through this type of forum.

The main benefits of using a group approach to continuous improvement are:

- A sharing and aligning of ideas. The old adage that 'two heads are better than one' applies.
- Involvement – people who feel consulted are more willing to make suggestions to improve the way things are done. As they work at the coalface they often have better, more practical ideas than managers.
- Ownership – people are more likely to implement ideas that they feel they have developed themselves than those that were developed elsewhere and imposed on them.
- A spin-off benefit is that involvement in the groups is developmental in its own right.

The downside of course is that these groups do take people away from their jobs. However, if an idea is implemented wholeheartedly the time lost should be regained quite quickly. Those organizations referred to earlier, which developed steering groups to oversee the introduction of Investors in People, were often organizations that already had improvement groups in place and were merely extending their use. Others may have been encouraged to develop a steering group by their consultant/advisor.

Following recognition many organizations that had such a steering group in place have started to use the group to oversee continuous improvement in relation the 'Investors' processes. Many of the case studies later in this book – Raflatac Limited, Barnsley Community and Priority NHS Trust, Queen Elizabeth's Boys School, and so on – illustrate how the use of groups has led to improvements in processes such as induction, communications, etc.

Developing improvement groups

When introducing the concept of improvement groups it is important to decide what they are expected to do. In order to maximize the benefits it is also vital that those involved are trained, developed and supported by their managers as appropriate. Many organizations train people to use improvement tools and techniques. Quite often the focus is on problem-solving techniques such as brainstorming, the use of fishbone diagrams or mind-maps. Others train participants in facilitation skills and other advanced communications skills.

Some organizations ask for volunteers to become involved in the groups, others may encourage involvement and occasionally, because a particular expertise is needed, the encouragement may be quite strong. The number of volunteers that come forward can in itself be a measure of the organizational culture. If, when introducing the concept of groups, only a few people initially seem to want to volunteer, the important message is don't give up – eventually the benefits will become apparent and more volunteers will come forward. It is also important here to emphasize the necessity of ensuring that people – at all levels – can see the links between what was intended and what the outcomes are. In other words, they embody the Investors in People philosophy without necessarily ever having heard of it!

Continuous improvement: the issues

Communications

Communications is one of the agreed core themes of Investors in People. Consequently, most organizations have reviewed and introduced new processes when implementing Investors in People action plans. Once they have been recognized as an Investor in People and given feedback by the assessor it is easy to adopt the approach that the systems are working and concentrate on other issues. (Hence, among other things, the need to keep a 'champion' after initial recognition as pointed out in the HPC Industrial Products case study in *Investors in People Explained*, 1999.)

However, when people are asked for suggestions for issues to be examined for further improvement the subject of communications is always mentioned. It seems self-evident that no matter what an organization does, there will still be a call for an improvement to communications, often accompanied by the lament that there is too much information and too little communication.

All this does not mean that organizations should not persevere. Our experience of those that don't review communications processes on a regular basis has demonstrated that complacency creeps in. For example organizations may *assume*:

- That processes are working effectively.
- That everyone is included.
- That because the systems are working that people *understand* what is being said.
- That people are (still) interested.
- That the *presentation* of the message by briefers is effective, ie that they will *automatically* make it 'bespoke' and relevant to the needs of their people if, for example, the MD changes or the currency strengthens. It only becomes 'bespoke' if the local line managers are able to link issues to the experience of their people.
- That sending out information is the same as communication.

Sometimes in the rush to inform people, many are over-informed. There may be too much communication and/or too much paperwork. When organizations have a number of part-time staff or staff who work out of the office a great deal, communications in person often becomes more difficult and they frequently fall back on paper communications. Unfortunately part-time staff do not get a part-time proportion of paperwork and the reading file gets piled high.

Another phenomenon has now emerged as a means of getting across messages – the use of e-mail. It is often a very effective method of getting consistent messages to staff quickly but again it can lead to too much information if not managed effectively. It is quite common for part-time staff or those working away from the office (and not linked by modem) to have a huge number of messages waiting for them on return – and then have to sift them out in terms of importance and urgency, if they have the time.

Evaluating communications processes is therefore very important. Surveys are often used to do this but it is equally effective to establish an improvement group to examine and comment on the strengths and weaknesses of current processes. They may even be used as a sounding board to establish such basic questions as:

- What do people *need* to know?
- What do people *want* to know?
- Who defines what counts as *need*?
- How is this done?

Matching what people need to know and what they want to know is probably the most difficult challenge that faces managers. Just like Sir Humphrey Appleby in the classic series *Yes Minister* – 'I need to know everything in order to know what I need to know' – some people will want to know everything while some will not be interested in anything. Balancing these two extremes should be made easier by having a communications group. Equally important is the checking that messages are really being understood. While managers have a role to play here, a communications group can act as an honest broker – especially if staff are reluctant to let managers know that they don't really understand. This can often be the case where employees are very junior, 'distant' from the core business, or where there is little attempt to communicate in a relevant way using appropriate language.

Processes that manage training and development

Organizations using Investors in People to develop processes to manage training and development may have introduced a range of systems where there is some overlap. Sometimes the systems involve a number of stages that are not seen, and therefore not used, as a cohesive package. The post-recognition stage is a time to review these processes and streamline them. If the opportunity is not taken to review them the danger is that they may fall into disuse as they may be too complex or overly bureaucratic. In our previous books we have pointed out that some paper-based systems may be needed to establish a discipline but, once established, the paper system can be made redundant. The areas for 'redundancy', potential duplication and lack of cohesion that the authors have seen involve:

- Separate appraisal/development review processes and pre-event briefing pro formas – it is possible to reduce paperwork and duplication by reviewing the currency of objectives that may already have the information entered on documentation rather than writing it out again. This issue is explored further in Chapter 4. Indeed, there are many successful examples of paper-free appraisals from the perspective of the appraisee. As the process is outcome-oriented it falls to the line manager to take notes and agree a final working document with the appraisee. This is especially effective where the focus on the paper element is off-putting or worrying to groups of employees who are not used to paperwork, and can be revisited throughout the planning cycle. Having said that, the emphasis must still be on the ownership of the process by the member of staff being reviewed.
- Development review/competence profiling and personal development planning that are not as cohesive as they should be – if processes are developed over a period of time the coherence of the various processes may not always be obvious.
- Individual pre-briefing pro formas when a group pre-brief would have been adequate, eg when a whole team is attending the same event or if sharing coverage of workshops at a conference.
- Huge induction packs. While it may be necessary to have such packs, presenting them as a whole to a new starter can be very daunting.
- Training records held both centrally and locally.
- Potentially unnecessary paperwork to prove that activity took place, eg signed attendance sheets at courses.
- Evaluating everything.
- Number-crunching with no further action.

We have frequently seen very complex, 'all singing, all dancing' appraisal processes when a simple development review process would have been adequate and more appropriate in some working environments. (Remember, the Investors in People standard does not require an appraisal scheme.)

Quite often as systems are developed it is easy to overlook earlier ones that may have been adopted in some areas but not in others. This can sometimes lead to duplication but may also lead to inconsistencies. An example seen recently in an organization involved the designing of functional competencies, the introduction of qualifications that involved assessment against set criteria and a set of skills handbooks that had partly fallen into disuse. While some criteria matched there were many that didn't. Sometimes it takes an outsider to spot this type of duplication but if improvement groups were given the task of systematically reviewing processes it is probable that these issues would be picked up. Similarly, where organizations are subject to a variety of inspections, assessments and audits they can often develop parallel systems, such as evidence collection and presentation, to accomplish the same task. Here the Investors in People process can be used to link together these activities.

Training and development actions

If organizations had not got end-of-course reaction sheets prior to initial recognition – sometimes called happy sheets (often that is all they confirm) – in place already, they will have introduced them. As with any type of evaluation it is not the evaluation itself that is important – it is what you do with the results. Part Three, 'Some Strategies and Tools', deals with a range of ways of selecting evaluation tools and what to do with the results.

Evaluating the evaluations and making the necessary changes contribute to continuous improvement. Piloting events or practice runs of presentations are other examples of evaluating and again the subsequent changes contribute to continuous improvement.

Experienced trainers point out that after evaluating a regular event two or three times, the format of the event will probably be OK, assuming notice is taken of the overriding messages that emerge. If that is the case there is no need to issue evaluation sheets to *everybody* at the end of *every* event; a percentage check should be sufficient. Again, the evaluation of everything is pointless.

Summary

This chapter has examined the issue of reviewing processes and development activities with a view to improving them by making them more cohesive. It started by reviewing the common feedback issues outlined by assessors following the first assessment. It looked at the indicator that relates to the concept of continuous improvement and went on to examine the issue of communications and training and development processes and gave illustrations of how some organizations have tackled them.

Note

1. Improvement groups have many different names, of course, but their typical function is to utilize the skill, knowledge and experience of people at various levels of the organization to add value in some specific context. In the words of the Vauxhall case study in the first two editions of *Investors in People Explained*, 'the people who do the job know the most about it'.

CHAPTER 4

Planning *for* Evaluation

This chapter looks at feedback issues around planning and evaluation. The most common comment that organizations make about Investors in People is that 'evaluation is the hardest part of Investors in People'. The authors disagree; we believe planning is the hardest part. Evaluation is easy if you were clear what you wanted at the planning stage. (In other words, objectives have been set.) The focus for this chapter is therefore planning *for* evaluation. The specific feedback issues picked up are:

- examining the quality of objectives at individual, team and organizational level; ensuring they are SMART (specific, measurable, achievable, realistic and timebound);
- increasing clarity about *planned* benefits especially at the organizational level;
- strengthening the links between business/organizational needs and training and development to reduce wastage, ie training that is not used;
- improving the quantification of benefits all round and the concomitant understanding of those benefits and their relationship to the planning process;
- increasing recognition of the benefits of the training and development activities.

It also continues the examination of the consolidation and cohesion issues discussed in the previous chapter: reviewing 'immature' planning processes to make them slicker and simple to administer, and reviewing complex and over-elaborate systems and systems that have no relevance.

Developing the linkages

When people first 'discover' Investors in People, a question they often ask is: *what's new about it?* Our answer has always been 'not a lot'.

The Investors in People process has been utilized and practised by thousands of organizations for almost a decade under the Investors in People banner. It is worth noting, though, that for many years prior to that, much of what Investors embodies has been practised by many organizations. However, what is perhaps new about Investors is the linkages that are implicit in the Standard. It is through these linkages that many organizations will realize most of the benefits. The initial linkage concerns the linkage between the business/organizational needs and the training/developmental need (see Figure 4.1). Although this linkage may well seem obvious, our experience shows that in practice these linkages are often quite weak. It is only when organizations are presenting their case for the assessor at the time of the first assessment that they realize the weakness of the linkage. It is not surprising therefore that the assessor gives feedback about strengthening the links. Improving the linkages will also lead to more effective and useful evaluation.

Developing the planning processes

A key part of the rationale underpinning Investors in People is that the Standard does not tell organizations how they should do certain things; it merely says *what* should be done. Therefore the assessors' role involves checking that processes that satisfy the Standard are in place and that they are working effectively. An experienced assessor will often observe that processes do not seem particularly good but if everyone says they are satisfied with them what can the assessor do? This is often the case with planning processes, especially for organizations that may have been urged to carry out

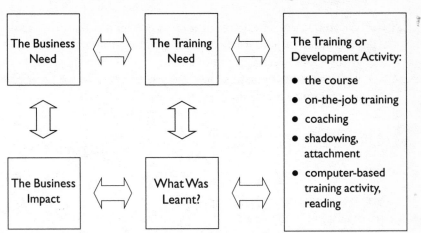

Figure 4.1 *The linkages*

'business' planning for the first time through their involvement with Investors in People.

The quality of business plans ranges from the barely adequate to the over-complex. Some plans are theoretically sound but quite impractical. We've seen small organizations with over 20 pages and large organizations with two or three pages. When it comes to drawing up a business plan it is important to decide why it is needed, how it will be used and who uses it.

Quite often at the first assessment the business planning process may be immature. Lots of lessons will have been learnt from the first attempt and frequently it may take two or three attempts to develop a process and format that an organization is comfortable with. Therefore for the first assessment an assessor may have to accept what may appear to be a barely adequate plan and give feedback suggesting that the planning process and layout is reviewed and refined.

The Investors in People Standard initially may seem quite clear about what is needed in order to meet the 'planning indicators':

2.1   A written but flexible plan sets out the organization's goals and targets.

2.2   A written plan identifies the organization's training and development needs, and specifies what action will be taken to meet these needs.

2.4   A written plan identifies the resources that will be used to meet training and development needs.

The first point is that the plans should be written. Although it is not always explicit, two other indicators do imply that plans should contain:

- A sense of direction (1.2 Employees at all levels are aware of the broad aims or vision of the organization); and
- SMART objectives/'training objectives' (2.6 Objectives are set for training and development actions at the organization, team and individual level).

However, it is when the evaluation objectives are examined that another dimension is added to planning:

4.3   The organization evaluates the contribution of training and development to the achievement of its goals and targets; and

4.4   Top management understands the broad costs and benefits of training and developing employees.

When trying to address the issues related to these two indicators, many organizations ask the question: 'What have we got out of the training and/or development?' rather than the question: 'What did we want from the training and development activity/investment?' If we examine Figure 4.1 again, we see that the vertical linkages between needs and outcome are the key ones when carrying out an evaluation. Our contention is that in order to make evaluation easier, at the *planning* stage you should be clear about what *difference* the training and development is *expected* to make, and what benefits are *expected* to be gained through the investment.

The evaluation question should then be simply: 'Did you get what you wanted?' (See Chapter 13, The Responsive Organization.) You may have got more than you wanted but on the other hand you may have got less than you wanted. If the latter is the case then further action is needed. The last point is important: evaluation should be useful and therefore is not just about successes. Evaluation should be precise and clear, with all stakeholders having been involved in agreeing what was wanted prior to any action being taken.

Planning for evaluation at the team level

There are still a significant number of organizations coming forward for reassessment that were assessed previously against an earlier set of indicators. These pre-1996 indicators were not as explicit about the 'team level' and consequently a number of these organizations do not present a strong case at this level.

The definition of what comprises a team is an issue for some organizations. A simple definition may be a group of employees who work together either casually, temporarily or permanently and have a common set of objectives. Examples of teams include permanent teams of workers such as the maintenance team, the 'management team' and shop floor or admin teams, etc. Branches, outlets, area/divisional offices, etc of large organizations are teams in this context. Casual or temporary teams may include project teams, improvement groups, etc.

The linkages illustrated in Figure 4.1 above can also be applied when identifying and planning the training and development needs of teams and evaluating the impact.

The use of the training matrix

There has been a recent resurgence in the use of training matrices. While they can be used for the identification of individual needs they are at their best when used in the team context, especially where multi-skilling is being introduced. Managers and team leaders/supervisors can see immediately whether they have sufficient people trained to be competent in the range of tasks that their team is responsible for carrying out.

However, the matrix can be used in much more sophisticated way, to illustrate an overall increase in skill levels within the team provided an element of assessment of competence is introduced by

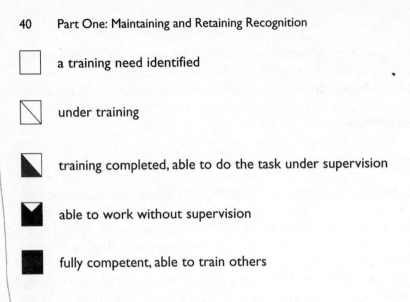

a training need identified

under training

training completed, able to do the task under supervision

able to work without supervision

fully competent, able to train others

Figure 4.2 *Symbols of competence*

introducing symbols rather than ticks. For example, you could use the symbols in Figure 4.2 to rate the level of competence of each employee.

The authors have found that as employees become more empowered they are encouraged to be involved in the development and completion of the matrix. Where this happens they have become more motivated and more willing to learn new tasks because they can see why it is necessary. It also helps with communicating training and development opportunities. It can help manage the 'wish list', ie training that an employee has asked for as an individual which is unlikely to take place as they can see that there are sufficient people trained to do the task to meet the needs of the team. They may not like it but at least they can understand it!

Planning for evaluation at the individual level

When they come forward for assessment, most organizations have realized the importance of the need to have a process that regularly reviews the training and development needs of individuals. They have also developed a process to ensure managers agree objectives with staff before training and development activity and debrief them afterwards. Frequently a form has been developed to assist with the process. The feedback given about the overall process usually concerns the quality of its application. Poor evaluation at this level also stems from poor objectives so the comment about SMART objectives is again relevant.

However, a quite frequent comment concerns the complexity of some of these processes. As illustrated in the Brodeur A Plus case study later in this book, complex processes often fall into disuse by busy managers. In Chapter 3 we talked about examining the bureaucracy – duplications and overlaps of processes. We would like to examine this further in relation to the above points.

One organization one of the authors worked with recognized the duplication and set about addressing it by designing one form that could address all the requirements. An adaptation of this form has been reproduced as Table 4.1. The idea behind the form is that it can be used as part of a structured training-review process and informally on an ongoing basis. The individual is empowered to complete columns 1 and 2 and discuss them with their line manager to agree the methodology which is then entered in column 3. Prior to the event, columns 1 and 2 would be reviewed to ensure the activity is still needed and make any adjustments to the objectives. Following the event the form is used as a debrief immediately afterwards to review whether what was learnt met the objectives. It is used some time after the event, either informally or as part of the next training review meeting, to check the impact. Individuals are encouraged to keep the form which is their personal plan and over a period of time the forms will provide a personal record of achievement which may have a number of uses, eg continuous professional development (CPD) record, to demonstrate an aspect of competence (ie been trained!). A range of other processes relating to looking at the impact of training and development can be found in Part Three, especially Chapter 11.

Introducing competence statements

Organizations are increasingly introducing statements of competence against which managers and individuals can agree areas of strength and development needs. Apor Limited, one of the first organizations to be recognized in 1991, introduced a simple system

Table 4.1 *Personal development plan*

To be completed before the development of the activity		To be completed after the activity	
1 What training do I need to do my job better?	2 What will I be able to do differently?	3 Methodology, who involved, eg on the job, a course, shadowing, computer-based training, etc	4 What was learnt? Objectives met?	5 Has performance improved? How?

which it called its competence assessment and action programme (CAAP). This system originally consisted of 32 performance areas under which a number of simple competence statements were listed. The statement related to different levels of performance expected by a person in a particular role. For example, under the heading 'verbal communication' the statements were:

1. answers questions, joins in social discussions;
2. explains instructions, information and ideas on a one-to-one basis;
3. explains instructions, information and ideas clearly in small groups;
4. strives to understand the audience's abilities and can explain complex information simply and clearly, avoiding jargon.

The competence purists may not like these statements but they at least represent a beginning and encourage people to think about assessing themselves and others objectively against agreed criteria. Apor Limited has revised many of the statements over the years and the process is still operating. The development of competency statements often leads to the use of NVQs but, if you are not keen on NVQs, you can use the performance criteria as competency statements and avoid reinventing wheels.

The use of competency statements for assessing people's abilities and performance can be used to strengthen evaluation at the individual level. They can also be used to strengthen evaluation at a team or organizational level, eg by using the initial assessment level as a benchmark and demonstrating that the overall competency grading has risen over a period of time.

Summary

This chapter has looked at feedback issues concerning planning and evaluation. It has contended that evaluation can be made easier if planning was carried out more effectively with the development of SMARTer objectives. It has examined planning for evaluation at the organization, team and individual level and demonstrated how simple competency statements can be used to enhance the quality of evaluation.

CHAPTER 5

The Continuing Role of Managers

This chapter examines the continuing role of managers (ie anyone who manages the training and development of people such as supervisors/team leaders etc). In particular it picks up the feedback issues of:

Further development of managers

- refreshing and updating management skills;
- examining the appropriateness of competences, the management NVQs, etc to ensure managers are clear about what is expected of them;
- where organizations have empowered their staff, ensuring that managers do not abdicate their responsibilities;
- encouragement where appropriate to be more proactive in encouraging people to identify and take up training and development opportunities.

It also addresses such feedback issues as:

Adding clarity

- increasing the involvement of people;
- giving a higher profile to *development* as opposed to training;
- further definition of roles and responsibilities, eg managing training and development;
- defining management 'effectiveness';
- expanding the 'buzz' from the shop floor to include the office areas;
- reducing the dependency on auditing or policing systems to ensure compliance by ensuring systems become part of the organizational culture;
- integrating what may appear as 'Investors in People processes' into the existing business or organizational processes.

The theme of the further development of managers is picked up a number of the case studies later in this book:

- Barnsley Community and Priority Services NHS Trust;
- Bidwells – where it involved a change in management style;
- Brodeur A Plus – who developed their own professional excellence programme;
- Raflatac Limited.

The continuing commitment of managers

We have been very consistent in – and insistent on – stressing the importance of the actions of managers in helping their organizations *achieve* Investors in People recognition. Without the continuing commitment of managers, the *maintaining* of recognition will be endangered.

We know that managers continue to be a very battered and bruised species. There are fewer of them, they have jobs to do as well as managing people and their development. Some managers see the management of people as part of their job whereas others see it as extra work. There are various gradations between these two opposites, and most organizations have managers who reflect the full range. Some managers are very effective at managing people; others are not. Some managers invariably make time for people while others struggle to find the time. Why is this often the case? The answer is *commitment*!

When defining the word 'commitment' the *Oxford Dictionary* uses the words 'dedication' and 'pledge' to an 'obligation' or 'cause'. These words imply having a belief. Our experience has shown that managers' belief in training and development of people stems from two sources: believing that training and development is an important part of their role; and believing there are great benefits derived from ensuring their people are trained and developed. The two sources are not mutually exclusive. All managers would probably agree with both statements but many would not go out of their way to ensure people are trained and developed because they merely say they believe in it rather than demonstrate that they believe in it.

People are very good at recognizing whether a manager is committed to their development or not. Assessors are frequently told by employees that 'their managers say they are committed' or that their 'manager is committed but work gets in the way, or until they have to put their hand in their pocket' and so on. Of course work will get in the way, but if it were a regular occurrence then people would question their commitment.

If an organization has been recognized as an Investor in People why are we still going on about commitment? Should this not have already been demonstrated to the assessor? The answer, annoyingly, is yes *and* no. Assessors have to make a judgement as to whether managers are supporting the training and development of their people. This support might well be carried out in a perfunctory and mechanical manner. Nevertheless, it is still done. The organization may well wish for some 'stretch' in this area as it continues to progress after the first recognition. Remember assessors have to give feedback if they decide an organization does not meet the Standard. Therefore they have to be very sure that something is not happening and can explain clearly what action is needed to address the gap.

The responsibility of senior managers

We have said that managers are a very battered and bruised species. It therefore falls to senior managers, who we concede may well be battered and bruised themselves, to review the needs of managers within the organization. This review may ask:

- Are there genuine reasons for the managers feeling the way they do?
- Are they clear about their role? Has it been defined clearly?
- Does it need re-defining?
- Are they actually doing what is agreed for them to do with regard to supporting their people? (This might be addressed in their own review/appraisal, for example.)
- Are the managers' people management skills and knowledge up to date?
- Am I offering sufficient support and feedback?
- Are systems too bureaucratic and elaborate?

Definition of management roles

In our previous book, *Investors in People Explained*, we described how the role of the manager has changed considerably. Our experience is that in many organizations this has meant adding to an already heavy workload with little taken away. We have often heard managers describe how they keep receiving more high-priority tasks but have little or no support with agreeing prioritization. Many organizations have introduced the concept of empowerment but frequently have not effectively examined the impact on managers. This has resulted in some managers actively seeking to maintain control and others losing control. Defining roles, levels of delegated authority, etc can help this process but quite often managers need specific coaching through this process so they in turn can coach their own staff who may be equally confused.

When it comes to managing the development of people in an empowered organization, our experience is that many managers leave it up to people to identify their own needs. This may work for some people but for others who are used to being encouraged and managed in a more 'hands on' way it can be disconcerting and ultimately dysfunctional. This applies equally to managers themselves. The key to overcoming this is to encourage discussion between individuals with the aim of agreeing expectations. (See Chapter 13, The Responsive Organization.)

Refreshing and updating management skills

Many organizations that have achieved recognition as an Investor in People will of course have managers who have been trained and developed but this may have been some time ago. The changing roles and expectations outlined above could lead to managers themselves requiring further training and development. While many management techniques may not have changed, some have, and this leaves more mature managers at a disadvantage when dealing with less experienced managers who may be more aware of the newer techniques, some of which may merely be old techniques which have been retitled.

The biggest change facing the more experienced managers has been that in management style. In essence, this is the move from management to leadership. Those managers who are more comfortable with the traditional management style are often faced with uncomfortable choices. The most positive approach involves coaching, mentoring, attendance at developmental events or perhaps exposure or short secondments to organizations that are very effective at employing the modern management techniques.

Defining effectiveness

In the previous chapter we discussed briefly the issue of competences. While many organizations have examined the use of the management standards many others have not. Again, to avoid reinventing wheels, it may be useful for organizations to use the competences but not go forward for the NVQ. This will often help clarify the sometimes woolly definitions about what an 'effective' manager is and help define what the organization (and its senior managers) expect an 'effective' manager to do.

As more and more competences are introduced, many organizations are encouraging their managers, particularly at team leader/supervisor level to become qualified assessors. This often means that managers are trained and assessed against the NTO (formerly TDLB) standard D32/D33. One of the case study companies, Airedale Springs, took this a stage further and encouraged people (not just managers/supervisors) to become qualified instructors. Our observations are that this contributes significantly to the development of better 'people managers'. As managers begin to take their responsibilities for developing people more seriously we have also noticed managers being trained and assessed as coaches against NTO standard C25.

Development versus training

Many organizations that have come forward and been recognized as Investors in People have done so on the back of training programmes. Some have reintroduced training having allowed it to lapse while others may have recently become convinced of the benefits of training people.

The issue for these organizations is that the focus may need to shift from training to development. In our book *Managing for Investors in People* we explore the issue of what constitutes development and the line manager role in promoting a culture of learning. Development activities include:

- reading/researching – reports, books, magazine articles, etc;
- videos, audiotapes, computer-based training, interactive video, etc;
- discovery learning;
- observing, questioning, listening, thinking/reflecting, reviewing mistakes;
- delegating, shadowing, visits, attachments/secondments, deputizing;
- job swaps, job rotation, rotating duties, eg chairing meetings;
- attending meetings or other types of discussion groups: quality circles/improvement groups;
- special projects;
- attendance at conferences, exhibitions.

Evaluating development

As far as possible, development should be a planned and structured set of activities. Inevitably unplanned development opportunities will occur and it would be bad practice in many cases not to seize these opportunities.

As indicated earlier, planning means setting objectives and agreeing a purpose so that evaluation can take place. An example of an objective/purpose may be to take on new or different responsibilities in order to test potential or encourage creativeness. Planned development should be structured, ie each step should be a building block to the next step, thus forming a development programme. This links into personal development planning as outlined in the previous chapter.

Because development may be less tangible or quantifiable than a classroom-based instructional style training programme, evaluation is clearly going to be more difficult. Evaluating the development programme may make it easier. The development plan can again be used or, where organizations have appraisal processes, this seems to be the obvious place to review the programme against its objectives/purpose. The following appraisal or periodic review would be an opportunity to monitor progress or evaluate the learning and effect on performance. Again, many of the techniques and strategies outlined in Part Three can help here, see especially Chapter 13. Organizations that have gained real benefits from Investors in People have strong cultures of development as opposed to training, and managers have the key role in promoting and supporting this culture.

Embedding

Although the systems and processes ideally should be embedded into the culture by the time the organization is assessed for the first time, as indicated in Chapter 1, frequently they are not. One of the reasons behind this is that many people still see Investors processes as separate from the normal 'management' processes.

This was illustrated quite recently when one of the authors carried out a reassessment during which it emerged that the organization carried out audits for ISO 9000, quality audits in relation to their implementation of the business excellence model and a regular 'mock' assessment to ensure compliance with Investors in People processes. This was overkill! Many of the activities were duplicated. That they are seen as separate reinforces the fact that Investors is often viewed as something extra – an additional burden, a bolt-on activity, etc. As it happened this was not a problem with the organization's reassessment as the people development culture was so strong. However, there are considerable savings in both time and other resources to be gained by merging the audits. Many sectors, such as education, are subject to a wide variety of reviews, assessments, inspections and audits. Here the message is even clearer: 'one size fits all'. The organization should be able to say, 'This is what we do, this is how we do it, this is how we check it works and this is what we do as a result of the checks.'

Ideally of course internal audits should be unnecessary if the processes are part of the culture and managers are committed to developing their people. Perhaps this is too idealistic but the authors believe this should be the aim.

Summary

This chapter has considered the changing and continuing role of managers in managing the training and development of people. In particular it has identified some of the challenges facing managers and how some organizations have supported them through these changes.

The chapter has also examined how some organizations have clarified the roles and expectations of managers with the use of competences and the management standards. Finally it reviewed the managers' role in promoting a culture of development and learning.

CHAPTER 6

Retaining Investors in People in Large and Multi-site Organizations

Implementing Investors and assessment against the Investors in People Standard has proved much more difficult with large and multi-site organizations. This chapter examines the 'maintenance' and post-recognition review issues that face large organizations, most of which have adopted different approaches to implementing the Standard. As the issues are complex for this type of organization it starts by examining the latest assessment guidelines from Investors in People UK concerning large and multi-site organizations. It then examines approaches to whole organization recognition that bring together individual units who have been recognized under the 'building-block' approach.

The background

Since Investors in People was first launched there have been a number of attempts to develop workable and meaningful guidelines that would encourage large and multi-site organizations to commit to Investors in People. The guidelines needed to ensure the process was rigorous but fair; costs against benefits. While the guidelines have been changed, the changes have not been substantial but this has added to the difficulties for these organizations, particularly for assessors, when they have come forward for reassessment.

The latest review of the guidelines took place during late 1997 and, following consultation with the stakeholder, were revised once again. Before looking at the implications for organizations coming forward for reassessment we have summarized the new guidelines below. They were agreed by the Board of Investors in People UK in May 1998.

Organization recognition strategies

The Investors in People UK Board confirmed the findings that:

> The Investors in People Standard is about the top management of whole organizations integrating their business strategy, business planning, and development of people to achieve improvements in their business performance. Only by working with this approach will organizations secure for themselves, and for the national economy, the maximum possible competitive advantage. The Standard is not about fragmented parts of larger organizations with limited delegated authority and autonomy achieving recognition as a mark of their own separate conformity to the Standard. Such an approach is likely to have limited organizational benefits; be expensive in terms of assessment; and cause public confusion regarding the use of the Investors in People 'badge'. It is for these reasons that organizations of whatever size or complexity should be encouraged to work towards recognition as Investors in People as whole organizations.

The options

For those large and multi-site organizations that wish to proceed, the revised guidelines set out two options: work towards the Standard as a whole organization or employ the building-block approach.

What is the 'whole organization'?

In most cases, the boundaries of the whole organization will be clear (eg a county council, a government department, a chain of building society branches, a chain of supermarkets, a university).

However, in some cases with complex holding company arrangements, it will be necessary to try and build as full a picture as possible of the ownership of the organization wishing to work with the Standard. At an early stage advisors are encouraged to check with the next level up in the ownership chain to find out whether a strategy is in place or being considered. If the parent organization does not wish, at this stage, to work with the Standard but gives the subsidiary organization its authority, then the lower-level organization can come forward for assessment and seek recognition. This organization can then be defined as the 'whole organization' for the purposes of this guidance.

The overall recognition strategies

Organizations wishing to work towards recognition using the building-block approach are encouraged to agree an overarching recognition strategy with the lead TEC/LEC/T&EA/Investors in People UK (normally a 'lead TEC' is the TEC nearest an organization's head office). The purpose behind an overarching recognition strategy is to help ensure that:

- eventually all parts of the organization will be covered by the Investors in People Standard;
- the organization works with the Standard in a cost-effective way;
- other TECs/LECs understand how the organization intends to work with the Standard and are able to work in partnership with the whole organization.

The overarching recognition strategy should be a 'living' document signed-off by an appropriate senior person at the top of the whole organization, usually by the chief executive (or equivalent) who is in effect giving authority for the subsidiary(s) to work towards the Standard. It should be reviewed regularly (at least once each year) and revised as the organization changes and as the organization's experience of working with the Standard grows.

The strategy should set out:

- which building blocks within the whole organization will be coming forward for assessment, and over what period of time;
- an agreement on how the organization intends to use the Investors in People logo for building blocks that achieve recognition. The use of the logo should not imply recognition for those parts of the organization not recognized;
- the chosen option for post-recognition review where appropriate, to be used by recognized building blocks, to maintain momentum prior to recognition of the whole organization.

The building-block approach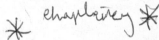

This approach was developed in response to the growing view that the responsibility for progression should rest with the organization. One of the authors was closely involved with the development of a model that anticipated the building-block approach – the Internal Quality Award. This model was used by higher education and the Church of England, among others. Readers interested in reviewing this model can access a description of the approach and look at the evidence matrix produced by Loughborough University's Pilkington Library (the first unit in the UK to achieve the award) on the Internet by visiting the following site:

http://www.lboro.ac.uk/service/sd/iipinhe/iipinhe.htm

Some large organizations may wish to move towards recognition on a subsidiary, departmental or divisional basis. This building-block approach is an acceptable way of working towards whole organization recognition and, wherever possible, should be managed within an overall recognition strategy.

When deciding which subunit can be termed a 'block', the organization will need to ensure that each subunit is able to develop its own:

- written but flexible plan that sets out the subunit's goals and targets;
- written plan that identifies the subunit's training and development needs, and specifies what action will be taken to meet these needs;

- written plan that identifies the resources that will be used to meet training and development needs.

Whole organization recognition

A whole organization cannot be recognized as an Investor in People until it has been assessed as a whole. Recognition of the whole organization depends – in addition to recognition of all of the building blocks – on strategic assessment by the lead assessor to confirm the senior management's commitment to Investors in People and its principles across the whole organization. The rationale for this strategic assessment is that the maximum benefits of Investors can only occur if it is seen and used as a strategic tool by the Senior Management. This strategic assessment, which can be carried out over a period of time, therefore comprises:

- a review of the organization's strategic plan and mission/vision or broad aims;
- a discussion with chief executive (or equivalent) to confirm the overall commitment to the principles of Investors in People within the whole organization;
- a follow-on discussion with other senior managers responsible for strategic planning, people issues and systems about how the principles of Investors in People are followed and applied across the whole organization.

It is important to note that the discussions with the senior managers at the centre of the organization are in relation to their responsibilities for the whole organization, not as heads of building blocks for which they may have been interviewed separately. In effect, this is a strategic assessment.

There are two ways in which an organization using the building-block approach can be recognized as a whole:

- During first assessment, when those parts of the whole organization not yet recognized come forward for assessment as one building block. This should be combined, if it has not already been carried out, with the strategic assessment of the senior management team. The lead assessor will consider the currency of evidence collected earlier in recognized units and seek additional evidence where appropriate.

- At the time of reassessment, when the whole organization comes forward for review rather than individual building blocks. Whatever review methodology is used (ie frequent review or less frequent – see page 21) it should include a strategic assessment of the senior management team.

In both cases, individual building-block recognitions may be exchanged for a single whole organization recognition.

Current practice

Since 1991 when Investors was first launched large employers have worked towards achieving recognition in a variety of ways. At one extreme there are employers who used the Standard as a framework to achieve change across the whole organization. At the other extreme some employers have allowed a particularly enthusiastic unit to commit and achieve recognition on its own with little impact on the rest of the organization.

From the start it was envisaged that, as the rationale for Investors was to improve business performance, large organizations would take a strategic approach to the Standard. This would involve top management integrating their business strategy, business planning and development of people to achieve business improvements.

In reality this has proved too bold a step for many organizations to take in one go. Top management were uncertain about the benefits and wanted some real experience within their own organizations before going further. Other organizations were devolving power away from the centre and wanted to avoid indicating centralist dictates about Investors in People. Some, although still having a strong centralist focus, found the task of getting all the organization up to standard for a single assessment too big a task, at least for the first assessment.

Through working with these organizations Investors in People UK and the delivery network have developed the approach to reflect these issues and have tried to tailor any recommendations to meet particular needs. However, they remain committed to developing a strategic approach to implementing Investors in People with the organizations they work with.

Maintaining the Standard

Many of the issues described earlier in this book apply to large and multi-site organizations; it is just the scale of the task that is different. The larger the organization the greater the reliance on managers to keep the momentum going. As indicated earlier many managers may not feel that benefits have been gained, especially for the managers themselves, and therefore any enthusiasm established during the run-up to the first assessment may disappear after the recognition. In large organizations there will always be success stories somewhere so the issue becomes one of communication. Communicating, sharing the benefits, any good practice, new ideas, etc is vital. It will reaffirm the commitment but also encourage some managers to persevere with the practices that may have been introduced or in some cases reintroduced.

Senior managers often visit local units so they should be encouraged to include Investors on their agenda when carrying out such visits. As well as reaffirming their commitment, it reminds managers that Investors has not gone away just because the organization has been recognized. Confirming the *continuing* commitment is as important post-recognition as communicating the original commitment was during the original implementation of Investors in People.

The implications for reassessment

Many organizations that originally adopted a unit-by-unit approach to implementation and assessment are moving towards achieving recognition for the whole organization. They are also resolving the corporate and strategic issues identified in earlier assessments. For example, when moving the assessment to a higher level within organizations (see Benefits Agency below), the assessor will be seeking strategic linkages between the higher and lower levels that may not be examined at the lower level. Where linkages do exist the focus may change when assessing at the higher level, eg the internal customer/supplier relationship between a head office and local office or manufacturing unit. Recognized organizations, or recognized units of organizations, must be reassessed and re-recognized before the expiry of the recognition, ie at least every three years.

Moving from the building-block approach to whole organization reassessment is quite complicated. Some organizations are therefore taking a staged approach. For example, the Benefits Agency assessments were originally on the basis of individual offices. Restructuring of the agency led to a focus on district level. The agency is now moving towards reassessment, directorate by directorate. This is the intermediate stage to a final single assessment in due course for the whole organization. It will be possible to achieve cost efficiencies in moving from one level to another by rolling up some of the later lower-level assessment with the overall assessment.

Other emerging issues

In large company-wide assessments, in the interests of ensuring a realism about costs, the majority of the units will not even be visited by the assessors. There is always the risk that some of those not sampled may not be up to the Standard. While some employees may feel short-changed by this process and devalue the recognition internally, it can also lead to problems at reassessment if these units are visited by the assessor. To avoid this happening it is recommended that external assessment is underpinned by strong processes for internal audit, quality assurance, employee attitude surveys, etc. The continued use of internal advisors after recognition can help monitor the continuing application of Investors particularly where the advisors carry out 'audits' of each other's areas. University College Northampton, recognized in 1997, has developed its own internal audit team. This team received top-up development to enhance their skills and knowledge in relation to Investors in People. The team, the membership of which changes over time to encourage wider participation, conducts audits across the full range of activities. In essence, the University College Northampton experiences a series of Investors in People-style internal assessments over the three-year period. Organizations like this, with their own strong internal audit function, would seem ideally placed to benefit from the revised review structure and, more importantly, to maintain and retain Investors in People as a central part of their normal operating practices and procedures. Once again, one size fits all!

Summary

This chapter has examined the issues that face large organizations as they strive to maintain the Standard. It has also described how large organizations are implementing strategies to merge post-recognition reviews (reassessments) of local units which will lead to whole organization recognition.

CHAPTER 7

The Indicators Re-explained

In this chapter we examine the indicators and note any points where the emphasis may be different at the reassessment stage. We review their original purpose and remind readers how they link and overlap with one another. We detail what an assessor will look for at the reassessment stage and how audit trails link in. The complete list of the indicators is included as Appendix 1.

The chapter goes on to show how the indicator concerning continuous improvement is especially applicable to organizations that are due for reassessment and links into all the clusters of indicators. Finally it reviews the need for written evidence at this stage.

Background

One question often asked about reassessment concerns the degree to which an organization has improved during the period between assessments. Ideally of course all organizations would like to improve and prosper and so would the country at large. That is one of the reasons Investors in People was created. However, Investors is not a panacea for everything that organizations face. Improvement is a relative commodity. Could an organization that has seen a substantial part of its market disappear but has survived be seen to have improved? Could organizations that are struggling because of currency fluctuations and laying people off be seen to be improving? As well as being a business development framework, Investors is also a useful model for managing change.

At the reassessment stage assessors will be looking for evidence that the use of the Investors model has continued. They will continue to look for evidence for each and every indicator. However, as the period between assessments may vary under the new proposals, the depth to which assessors will probe certain areas and the way in which evidence will be sought against the indicators will vary. Generally assessors will identify objectives for the assessment based on the 'audit trails' highlighted in Chapter 2:

- changes in ownership;
- growth/decline;
- structure;
- senior management or key personnel;
- introduction of other quality or business development tools;
- changes to markets/new products;
- introduction of IT/new legislation;
- changes to key processes.

The need for written evidence

It may be worth reviewing this point again. At the time of writing many organizations coming forward for reassessment, especially those that have waited the full three years, are still producing portfolios. The reasons for this vary. For example, sometimes the person preparing for reassessment is not the same person who prepared the case for the first assessment and they therefore found it useful to go through the portfolio-building process. One such person said, because they had built up a portfolio, even they were surprised to see how much the organization had achieved during the three years.

At this point we would like to reiterate the point that portfolios are not necessary. The new model emphasizes this point and the fact that the only indicators that must be met by written evidence are those concerned with planning (2.1, 2.2 and 2.4). When applying for a post-recognition review the only documentation requested is concerned with planning. No storyboard is requested as the change pro forma serves that purpose. The assessor will also be provided with a copy of the previous assessment report. Some organizations offer to give a presentation to bring the assessor up to date with changes or, in the case of assessors new to organizations, to brief them and perhaps show them round the premises.

For reassessment there is no requirement for organizations to give an indicator-by-indicator explanation of how they think they meet the Standard. It is up to assessors to match what they find with the indicators.

The indicators themselves will be revised over the next year. Nevertheless, the focus of Investors in People is still the same and whatever format the indicators take (they may be more outcome-oriented), it is still a very useful exercise to analyse them in this context.

Looking at the indicators

We remind readers that they should continue to view the Standard in a holistic way. We have therefore grouped the indicators under six key elements:

- planning and monitoring for the organization;
- planning and monitoring for teams and individuals;
- commitment and communications;
- managing training and development;
- evaluating the effectiveness of the actions for teams and individuals;
- evaluating the effectiveness of the actions for the organization.

Planning and monitoring for the organization

The focus of the trails concerns change, and changes imply a need for some kind of retraining or further development. The starting point for the assessor at reassessment will therefore be the planning process. Additionally, as indicated in earlier chapters, much of the feedback from the first assessment often concerns the need for SMARTer objectives in order to improve the quality of evaluation. This also suggests an emphasis on the planning processes.

The relevant indicators

1.2   Employees at all levels are aware of the broad aims or vision of the organization.

2.1   A written but flexible plan sets out the organization's goals and targets.

2.2   A written plan identifies the organization's training and development needs, and specifies what action will be taken to meet these needs.

2.3   Training and development needs are regularly reviewed against goals and targets at the organization, team and individual level.

2.4   A written plan identifies the resources that will be used to meet training and development needs.

Original purpose

This group of indicators sets the context both for the development of the organization and the development of its people. Investors in People is about developing people to help achieve the organization's goals and targets. It is not about having a large training budget, or always saying 'yes' to people's training requests. Training and development must be closely focused on the organizational needs now and into the near future.

Indicator 1.2 has been included here because developing the broad aims or vision is essential for the success of any organization as the first part of the planning process. The only indicators that must be demonstrated to the assessor as written evidence concern the planning process. That does not mean that every organization has to have detailed plans that analyse every eventuality but it should show clear goals and targets, measurable as much as possible, and the timescale over which they are to be achieved. Starting with measurable goals and targets provides the base for the monitoring and evaluation of organizational performance, and its importance cannot be overemphasized. Some may be hard financial measures; others could be measured in terms of perhaps customer or employee satisfaction or reduced wastage rates. The questions to ask are: 'How will we know we are being successful? What should we be doing to improve?' You may find that a number of people in the organization at all levels come up with different and valuable ideas when the questions are posed this simply.

The emphasis of Investors in People is always on 'fitness for purpose', so small organizations would not be expected to produce the depth of analysis and detail appropriate to larger organizations. However, they would be expected to take a longer-term view even if this is only 12 months ahead. Larger organizations may have three- or five-year strategies.

Linked to this there should also be a plan that includes a 'people dimension' – identifying the broad skills and knowledge or changed organizational culture needed to achieve the organization's objectives (indicator 2.2). There should be evidence that the resources (ie time, people, money and facilities) are identified to ensure the 'people dimension' is achieved (2.4). The plan should also allow for contingencies – sudden changes that may also affect the skills and knowledge required from people so that more training and development, and perhaps resources, are needed to meet the revised targets (2.3). Defining success criteria will become more important as organizations come up for reassessment. If they have not got benchmarks against which to compare their performance, how are they going to demonstrate continuing improvement?

What an assessor will look for at reassessment

The first question is likely to be: 'Has the original planning process been developed in any way?' If the feedback from the first assessment concerned weak evaluation or understanding of the impact, costs and benefits of training and development, then assessors will be looking for improved objective setting. They may look to see if benchmarks or key performance indicators (KPIs) have been introduced as a means of improving evaluation of the impact and the benefits.

Has there been any change to the vision or broad aims? How are the changes reflected in the written plan, the targets and goals and how they have been linked to the 'people dimension'? The assessor will also look for the continued linkage between achieving organizational goals and targets and the training and development needs identified, particularly where any of the changes highlighted earlier have implications on the training and development needs of the people. The assessor will look for evidence that the people plans continue to be resourced. This starts one of the original 'audit trails', which will demonstrate that evaluation takes place. Assessors will look for evidence that progress continues to be monitored and that the training and development needs of people are reconsidered where plans are changed.

Planning and monitoring for teams and individuals

The relevant indicators

2.3   Training and development needs are regularly reviewed against goals and targets at the organization, team and individual level.

2.5   Responsibility for training and developing employees is clearly identified and understood throughout the organization, starting at the top.

2.6   Objectives are set for training and development actions at the organization, team and individual level.

2.7   Where appropriate, training and development objectives are linked to external standards, such as National Vocational Qualifications (NVQs) or Scottish Vocational Qualifications (SVQs) and units.

3.4   All employees are made aware of the training and development opportunities open to them.

3.5   All employees are encouraged to help identify and meet their job-related training and development needs.

Original purpose

In spite of the perception of many people being to the contrary, Investors in People is not *just* about top-down planning. The purpose of this cluster of indicators is to ensure that the changes in skill, knowledge and attitudinal needs of teams and individuals are identified and taken into account by the plans of managers (team leaders, supervisors, etc). The indicators allow individuals to identify their own needs, usually in the context of organizational needs. They also point to the need for managers to be competent and effective. They demonstrate this competence in managing the training and development of their staff (see below). Again this cluster of indicators link directly to the evaluation indicators associated with teams and individuals.

Indicator 2.7 encourages organizations and line managers to consider the benefits and use of appropriate external qualifications. Achieving qualifications rewards individual achievement and it will add to an organization's credibility in terms of the skills and knowledge of staff in customers' eyes and provide an externally benchmarked measure of the organization's 'stock' of competence and capability. Among the external qualifications an assessor will expect organizations to have considered are NVQs or SVQs, as well as appropriate national technical or professional certification.

What an assessor will look for at the reassessment

During the course of general discussion assessors will ensure that teams and individuals are still clear who is responsible for their training and development (2.5). They will check that the process (or processes) that identified the needs of individuals and teams is still effective and has identified needs associated with any of the changes included in the organization's plan (2.3). They may also look to see if the process itself has been reviewed and if the review has led to any improvements (4.5). Assessors will expect to see that individual needs continue to link back to the needs of the organization. It does not have to be an appraisal process nor does it have to be written but *ideally* the outcomes should be adequately recorded so as to be effective over time.

Assessors will expect line managers to have continued to agree with teams and individuals prior to any activity, through briefings and discussion, what the training or development is for and how they will assess whether the training and developmental activities have been successful (2.6). Again if the quality of evaluation was an issue from the first assessment they will expect to see an improvement in the quality of training objectives. The assessor will also look for evidence that managers, on behalf of the organization, are still encouraging the use of external qualifications, or at least have continued to examine their relevance (2.7).

Commitment and communications

At the reassessment stage the emphasis shifts from top management being *committed* to them *continuing to be committed*. Change also implies a need for communication. A key part in managing change is keeping people informed about how it may affect them and what the organization will do to help them cope.

The relevant indicators

1.1   The commitment from top management to train and develop employees is communicated effectively throughout the organization.

1.2   Employees at all levels are aware of the broad aims or vision of the organization.

1.3   The organization has considered what employees at all levels will contribute to the success of the organization, and has communicated this effectively to them.

1.4   Where representative structures exist, communication takes place between management and representatives on the vision of the organization's future and the contribution that employees (and their representatives) will make to its success.

2.5   Responsibility for training and developing employees is clearly identified and understood throughout the organization, starting at the top.

3.4   All employees are made aware of the training and development opportunities open to them.

4.6   Top management's continuing commitment to training and developing employees is demonstrated to all employees.

Original purpose

The purpose of these indicators is to ensure that all employees are aware of what the organization is trying to achieve and how they can contribute to its success directly and through the enhancement of their skills. As well as being clear about their own role they should be confident that the organization will equip them with the skills and knowledge necessary to carry out their role. The commitment to ensure this happens starts at the top of the organization, by giving them an adequate priority to 'business'-led training and development, in the face of other organizational priorities. The commitment of senior managers will involve them encouraging line managers to demonstrate their commitment.

Continuing commitment (4.6) involves continuing to communicate to the people the contribution that training and development has made to organizational successes. This contribution will have been identified through the evaluation processes (see below). This message implies that the organization will continue to train and develop because it pays to do so. It will involve celebrating:

- the successful achievement of business objectives and *how training and development has contributed*;
- periodically reinforcing the benefits achieved from the spend on training and development;
- individual, or team, achievement of qualifications or other successes where training and development has contributed.

What an assessor will look for at reassessment

Do people believe that senior people are still committed to their training development? What does the senior team do to continue to demonstrate this commitment – is it only in words or in actions and resources?

An assessor will expect to find evidence that communication to reinforce the requirements of the above indicators has taken place at all levels in the organization, particularly in relation to any changes that have or will be occurring. Assessors will once again be checking on employee understanding. Much of the evidence for these indicators will continue to be verbal, from the site interviews.

The assessor will therefore ask questions to establish how staff have been kept informed about any changes that have taken place:

- If no changes have occurred, have they continued to be kept informed about what the organization expects to achieve?
- Can they explain it in simple terms and their part in helping that achievement?
- Are they still clear about their own role and if not who to ask, especially if they need further training and development?
- Do they continue to find out about training and development opportunities?

- When training and development is successful, are they encouraged to develop further? What future training and development plans does the organization have?
- How does this link to career development opportunities – lateral development as well as promotional?

Where there are recognized employee representative structures such as trade unions, staff associations, works councils or other employee representative committees, the assessor will check how they are communicated with or consulted about any changes to the organization's plans and kept up to date with feedback about its performance and the provision of relevant training and development to support this. This continues to be the only indicator that can be omitted if it is not relevant because such structures do not exist.

Managing training and development

The role of the line manager continues to be key to Investors in People. We have consistently argued that managers have a role in helping organizations meet *all* the indicators. This cluster of indicators examines, in particular, how the organization continues to identify and meet the training and development needs of its managers and how the managers apply that training and development, particularly in relation to 'people management'. This is particularly important as management style and managers' roles are constantly changing.

The relevant indicators

2.5 Responsibility for training and developing employees is clearly identified and understood throughout the organization, starting at the top.

3.1 All new employees are introduced effectively to the organization and all employees new to a job are given the training and development they need to do that job.

3.2 Managers are effective in carrying out their responsibilities for training and developing employees.

3.3   Managers are actively involved in supporting employees to meet their training and development needs.

3.5   All employees are encouraged to help identify and meet their job-related training and development needs.

3.6   Action takes place to meet the training and development needs of the individuals, teams and the organization.

Original purpose

- Has the organization identified who is responsible for training and developing employees?
- Is everyone clear about this responsibility (2.5 *and* 1.3)?
- Has the organization defined or redefined what it expects managers to do in order to be effective?
- Are the development needs of line managers identified and met (3.2), especially those new to the role?
- Do managers demonstrate their effectiveness by supporting the development of their people through maintaining and developing the 'learning climate' for their teams (3.3), and those teams and individuals continuing to take some responsibility (3.5)?
- Are new employees inducted effectively (3.1) to their job, the organization, its environment and systems?
- Similarly, are those existing employees who change jobs inducted effectively to their new jobs?
- Do they get any initial training they need?
- If jobs are changed or expanded, do people receive the training and/or development necessary to carry out the additional responsibilities?

What an assessor will look for at reassessment

Confirmation, either in writing or verbally, that the appropriate action has taken place and the manager's role in it. Because identified action will not always require a formal training course but takes place on the job, assessors will check that the line manager has continued to support through encouragement and coaching and the provision of adequate time and resource. In short, the assessor will expect a similar kind of continued commitment from line managers that is expected from the top of the organization to satisfy indicator 4.6 (and to an extent 1.1). This may mean, for example, the manager ensuring action takes place, in spite of other priorities, to achieve those skills and knowledge areas that were identified as necessary to meet the goals and targets of the business, and the needs of individuals. Where they exist, assessors may ask to examine centrally held training records or individual learning records, development plans, etc.

Evaluating effectiveness of actions for teams and individuals

As indicated earlier, much of the feedback from the first assessment often concerns the quality of evaluation. If this is the case the assessor will be seeking evidence that evaluation processes have been developed and improved. This should lead to an increased awareness of the impact of training and developmental activity on the achievement of the organization's plans.

The relevant indicators

2.3   Training and development needs are regularly reviewed against goals and targets at the organization, team and individual level.

2.6   Objectives are set for training and development actions at the organization, team and individual level.

3.6   Action takes place to meet the training and development needs of the individuals, teams and the organization.

4.1   The organization evaluates the impact of training and development actions on knowledge, skills and attitude.

4.2   The organization evaluates the impact of training and development actions on performance.

Original purpose
To check the effectiveness of the training and development actions on the performance of individuals and teams and identify areas for further improvement. Were the planned objectives achieved?

What the assessor will look for at reassessment

As indicated earlier the assessor will seek the 'audit trail' that demonstrates evaluation of the learning and the application of the learning. At this level the trail starts in one of two places: the training and development objectives set at the identification of training needs (eg at appraisal or whatever other method is used to satisfy indicator 2..3); or at the pre-event briefing or discussion (2.6).

The assessor will check that line managers, team leaders, etc have continued to clarify the purpose of the agreed action, ie what the person or team was expected to learn and what impact was expected from the application of the learning (2.3/2.6). They will then ask:

- Did the action take place (3.6)?
- Did the line manager check the planned learning was achieved (4.1)?
- Did they later check that the planned impact on the individual's performance was achieved (4.2)?

The questions will also be asked at the team level. Was it effective (4.1) and can the team now do what was expected (4.2)? As implied, the assessor will look for evidence of the continued use of post-event debriefing, whether formal or informal, to check what people think they can do, and subsequent evidence that line managers monitor the performance to check whether the training or development was successful. The appraisal or development review process should continue to play an important part in this process. As in the first assessment the assessor will expect use to be made of the evaluation evidence, for example what happens if performance does not improve? Is further training or development planned?

Evaluating effectiveness of actions for the organization

The relevant indicators

2.1   A written but flexible plan sets out the organization's goals and targets.

2.2   A written plan identifies the organization's training and development needs, and specifies what action will be taken to meet these needs.

2.3   Training and development needs are regularly reviewed against goals and targets at the organization, team and individual level.

2.6   Objectives are set for training and development actions at the organization, team and individual level.

3.6   Action takes place to meet the training and development needs of the individuals, teams and the organization.

4.1   The organization evaluates the impact of training and development actions on knowledge, skills and attitude.

4.2   The organization evaluates the impact of training and development actions on performance.

4.3   The organization evaluates the contribution of training and development to the achievements of its goals and targets.

4.4   Top management understands the broad cost and benefits of training and developing employees.

4.6   Top management's continuing commitment to training and developing employees is demonstrated to all employees.

Original purpose

At the organizational level the evaluation 'audit trail' starts with the business goals and targets (2.1) and their link to the objectives set for training and development (2.2). These evaluation indicators should help demonstrate that these objectives are being achieved.

Quite often it is apparent during the first assessment that senior management have evaluated the impact of training and development but without recourse to the original objectives. They may have tried to use the original objectives but have realized that the quality of objectives could be improved. As we said in our previous book *Investors in People Explained*, rationalizing the effect and the benefits after the event is not effective evaluation! Nor are loose references to an overall improvement in general business performance or other organizational indices. Comparing the outcomes against objectives is therefore essential to effective evaluation. By-products may have been gained and these can be noted but the basic premise is: this is what you hoped to achieve – did you?

In the interests of continuous improvement it is also important to look at the outcomes of the evaluation to see if the training activity or the processes themselves can be improved and if so, that these improvements are implemented (4.5).

What assessors will look for at reassessment

They will be looking for much the same as at the original assessment. Their expectations will probably be higher, however, especially where feedback has been given about the quality of the evidence of evaluation at the first assessment.

The assessors will look for evidence at the organizational (or global) level that the outcomes of the training and development have continued to be evaluated in terms of the broad learning that took place, and the impact on the business. It is not enough to describe the training activities and show business improvements without demonstrating the direct link between the two.

They will ask how plans, especially training and development plans, were monitored. How were they changed (2.3)? How effective were the changes?

The assessor will follow the audit trail starting at the broad aims (2.2) and/or the objectives (2.6), how the resource was used, through the action evidence to the evaluation of the effectiveness of that action.

They will then seek evidence of the impact of the organization as a whole (4.3). This implies, especially in larger organizations, that there is a process that collates the information gathered at the individual and team levels.

Finally the assessor will seek confirmation that the impact continues to be recognized at the senior management level so that a view can be taken as to the costs and benefits of the training and development (4.4); whether it had the desired impact on the achievement of the business objectives. The assessor will *expect* senior managers to be fully aware of both the cost *and* benefits of the investment in broad but measurable terms (4.4), and be able to offer illustrations. As mentioned earlier the assessor will seek evidence that this information has been used, ie communicated to the employees, to reinforce the continuing commitment of senior managers (4.6).

A final implication of the above is that you should be able to demonstrate evidence through the planning cycle from the identification of the business (or organizational) need, to the review at the end of the cycle. At the reassessment stage, just as at the first assessment, assessors generally accept that pure evaluation of the effect of training and development is almost impossible, as there may be many other factors that contaminate results. They will expect, however, that linkages are made that show the contribution training and development has made.

Continuous improvement

The relevant indicator

4.5   Action takes place to implement improvements to training and development identified as a result of evaluation.

Original purpose

As mentioned in earlier chapters, many people argue that this is unnecessary as continuous improvement is inherent in the Investors process. The fact that so many references to this indicator have been included in the descriptions above reinforces that point.

Our experience is that many organizations do not have to take special action to meet this indicator as they review and improve the way they do things without thinking about it. This is particularly true when organizations come forward for reassessment.

What assessors will look for at reassessment

It is more than likely that evidence will emerge from discussions and interviews with people from throughout the organization that training and development systems and processes have been evaluated and improved. The assessor will also look for evidence that shows how feedback from training and developmental events is used to improve subsequent events. If it concerns external provision the feedback may have led to providers not being used again. The use of feedback from the first assessment may also demonstrate that feedback is evaluated and used where relevant.

Summary

This chapter has examined the expectations of the assessor at the reassessment stage. It has reviewed the purpose and links between indicators in the context of reassessment. It has identified a number of clusters of indicators and audit trails, often involving *change* in one form or another, that assessors will seek to follow.

CHAPTER 8

Sources of Help

Once organizations have been recognized as Investors in People, the degree of help needed to maintain the Standard varies considerably. Our experience is quite often that those organizations that have opted for a three-year reassessment ask for help to review what they have done in case they have 'taken their eye off the ball'.

This chapter is included as a 'who's who' of the various sources of help available to assist organizations through the process. As addresses and telephone numbers can soon become out of date it does not give full details of all the sources. It does not attempt to list all sources but merely points to the key players who in turn may have their own sources to which they redirect anyone who wants to know more.

1. Investors in People UK

Investors in People UK was established in July 1993 as a private company limited by guarantee. It opened for business on 1 October 1993. Originally based in Sheffield it moved to premises at 7–10 Chandos Street, London W1M 9DE in April 1994. The role of Investors in People UK is:

- to guard, direct and take the lead on the development of the Investors in People National Standard;

- to define the assessment process in outline;
- national promotion and support;
- national quality assurance;
- assessment and recognition of national organizations, TECs & LECs.

Investors in People UK works in close consultation with all its partners. Investors in People UK also has a Web site – www.iipuk.co.uk

2. National training organizations (NTOs)

Every sector has its own NTO. The key remit is to address education, training and 'competitiveness issues'. They are planned to evolve into a single network that covers all industry and service sectors, the aim being to develop a 'strategic approach to enhance national and individual prosperity'. NTOs have a key role with regard to Investors in People – for example, joint projects, producing practical guides, case studies and other supportive sector specific material.

In 1997 the then Lifelong Learning Minister Kim Howells said that NTOs are:

> pioneers of a new concept: the first Government recognized training organizations. As such, you represent a new era of training for Britain. I look forward to forging a creative partnership between Government and NTOs, so we can develop a more strategic approach to the ways sectors influence education and training at national level.

One of the authors works for the national training organization for higher education (UCoSDA, see Point 4 below). Their first aim is to promote strategically planned, continuing and coherent staff development and training provision across universities and colleges in the United Kingdom. For further information about NTOs contact:

The NTO National Council
10 Amos Road
Meadow Court
Sheffield
S9 1BX
Tel: 0114 2619926

3. Training and Enterprise Councils (TECs)

Over the last few years some TECs have merged with Chambers of Commerce – a trend that is likely to continue – and have become known as Chambers of Commerce, Training and Enterprise (CCTEs).

At the time of writing the future of TECs is being reviewed. As they are the main local delivery network for Investors in People, any changes will need to take this into account and a new delivery network established.

TECs were set up by the government in the late 1980s to deliver products and services such as youth and adult training, establish education partnerships and generally support enterprise start-up in specific geographical areas throughout England and Wales. TECs are independent companies limited by guarantee and driven strategically by a board of directors drawn in the main from key people in local business communities but also from the public and voluntary sector. A board's role is to ensure that the portfolio of services offered meets the local needs. There are now 78 TECs working in partnership with other local organizations that are key players in the economic regeneration of their areas. They also have the task of encouraging employers to train and develop their existing workforce in order to develop the skill base on which the future prosperity of the country will be based, which is where Investors in People fits in. TECs are responsible for the local delivery of Investors in People. This means they are responsible for marketing and promotion, advice and guidance, assessment and recognition. TECs deliver this in a variety of ways. All receive funding from central government, mainly from the Department for Education and Employment, to help support enterprise activities. This budget has gradually been reduced and therefore financial support for Investors in People from TECs is limited and varies from one TEC to another.

The number of staff working on Investors in People also varies from TEC to TEC, with most using outside help to deliver the initiative. Later in this chapter the role of this outside help, mainly in the form of consultants, is described.

An increasing number of TECs are offering workshops or seminars that are geared to helping organizations through the process. Some TECs will offer these free and others will make a nominal charge. If nothing else, these workshops will introduce you to other organizations that are going through the process and will often be very willing to share ideas, problems etc.

One of the authors has been closely associated with West London TEC and an example of the workshops on offer there are:

- the line manager's role in Investors in People;
- the internal adviser;
- setting objectives, targets and standards for evaluation.

Other TECs will offer similar workshops.

4. The Universities' and Colleges' Staff Development Agency (UCoSDA)

The Universities' and Colleges' Staff Development Agency (UCoSDA) was created in 1989. It is one of the agencies of the Committee of Vice Chancellors and Principals and was recognized as the National Training Organization for Higher Education (THETO – The Higher Education Training Organization) in November 1997.

UCoSDA seeks to provide advice, support and resources to its member universities and colleges in the planning, organization, provision and evaluation of continuing professional/vocational development for all personnel in the higher education sector. It currently employs an approved Investors in People Assessor – one of the authors of this book. The UCoSDA philosophy captures some of the central themes of this book and is summarized as follows:

- investment in the personal, professional and vocational development of all staff employed by universities and colleges is fundamental:
  (a) to the successful achievement of organizational goals and
  (b) to the motivation and continuing capacity of individual staff members to support that achievement.

UCoSDA has produced a number of briefing papers and other publications on Investors in People and related issues and can be contacted at the following address:

Ingram House
65 Wilkinson Street
The University of Sheffield
Sheffield
S10 2GJ
Tel: 0114 282 4211
Fax: 0114 272 8705

5. Scotland – Local Enterprise Companies (LECs)

The position in Scotland is different. LECs were set up at about the same time as TECs but they have a wider remit, as they not only took over the delivery of products and services such as youth and adult training, but also embraced the role of the Scottish Development Agency and the Highlands and Islands Development Agency.

LECs are private companies limited by guarantee who are contracted to either Scottish Enterprise or Highlands and Islands Enterprise. There are 22 LECs although some counts might show 23, as one straddles the border between Scottish Enterprise and Highlands and Islands Enterprise and is often counted twice.

Assessment and recognition is carried out by Investors in People Scotland so the role of the LECs is to carry out the same work as TECs minus assessment and recognition. They too use outsiders to deliver various stages of Investors in People. The telephone numbers and addresses of LECs can be found in local telephone directories.

6. Investors in People Scotland

The role of Investors in People Scotland has been described in Chapter 7, The Recognition Process, in our earlier book, *Investors in People Explained*.

7. Northern Ireland: Training and Employment Agency (T&EA)

The Training and Employment Agency was established as an agency of the Northern Ireland Civil Service in 1990. It carries out a role similar to that of the Employment Department and Employment Agency in Britain (ie a training and job-broking service).

One of its divisions has a particular remit to support business and it is under this requirement that Investors in People sits. The agency has broadly the same role as the TECs in delivering Investors in People. However, the financial support offered by the T&EA is through its Company Development Programme and the consultants who deliver it.

8. Management Charter Initiative (MCI)

For information on the Management Standards or the booklets *Managing Business Success* and *The Good Managers Guide* contact MCI at the following address:

Russell Square House
10–12 Russell Square
London WC1B 5BZ
Tel: 0171 872 9000

MCI are also the management and enterprise NTO.

9. Consultants and consultancy organizations

Feelings about using consultants differ considerably from one organization (or person) to another. This section does not intend to debate the relative merits of using consultants. The arguments are well rehearsed elsewhere. However, because the resources within TECs and LECs are limited, most, if not all, use outside help to deliver the various stages of Investors in People.

Because TECs, LECs and T&EA are so reliant on using consultants, Investors in People UK have developed a quality assurance (QA) process for consultants and advisors who work with organizations on Investors in People. The process covers roles such as selling, diagnosing and developing action plans and implementing action plans. The quality assurance process is managed by a number of advisory registration units (ARUs) throughout the UK and approved by Investors in People UK.

The QA registration process for potential advisors involves sitting a written multi-choice examination followed by a situational interview in front of an interview panel. Investors in People took an interest in this subject as the credibility of the process of becoming an Investor in People was being affected by advice and guidance being given that was not as good as it should have been. There were a number of examples of assessments being deferred purely because of bad or misleading advice. Although deferrals still occur the number related to bad advice has reduced significantly. This was also the case with the former guidelines on authority and autonomy.

Choosing and using consultants

So what can be done if you want to use a consultant? The first stage is to have a discussion with someone from the Investors team at the local TEC or LEC. An important point is that you should be clear what it is you want the consultant to do. The next stage is to ensure that the consultant is qualified to deliver what you want, especially if you are approached directly by a consultant. This is probably easier said than done as there are so many consultants touting for work. The first question should be: 'Are they registered with Investors in People UK as consultant advisor? Through which ARU?' You can check that they are registered by visiting Investors In People UK's Web site (see address above). Some further simple questions you may ask are:

- How many companies have they helped to achieve recognition?
- Which TECs/LECs are they working with?
- What training have they had in connection with Investors in People?
- Are they an accredited assessor?
- How many assessments have they carried out?
- What is their approach to helping organizations achieve Investors in People status? (Beware those consultants who will get it for

you and have a sure-fire way of meeting a number of indicators! They may sell you a package that you don't want or need.)
- What sector expertise do they bring? In some cases having a sector expertise may save time with interpreting the Standard but it is not always essential.

An additional question may concern their experience of reassessments or helping organizations with their maintenance of the Standard

How consultants can help

Provided you get the right consultant they can help in a number of ways. First they may have experience working with TECs and may help you secure some financial support. They should have experience of carrying out certain tasks or have seen examples of different approaches in a cross-section of companies and can therefore help you avoid reinventing wheels.

Other organizations

The help offered by peers who have been recognized and perhaps maintained their recognition may prove valuable. The first organizations to be recognized and subsequently re-recognized were inundated by callers who wanted to know how they did it; some of them may well have wondered why they got involved. However, now there are a lot more people to offer this kind of guidance.

Most TECs and LECs invite representatives from recognized organizations to speak at local events so you may well find out about them then. If not, or if you need to identify a specific type of organization, your TEC or LEC will be able to help identify and put you in touch with someone who can help.

Investors in People material, videos, etc

Finally, there continues to be a wealth of material available to help you work through the various stages of the process. Most TECs have produced their own material but in addition there is a lot of nationally available material produced by Investors in People UK (a catalogue with their material and merchandise is available). There is also a lot of material in the form of articles in management and training magazines and books (this is one!) either being developed or already in existence to help form an understanding of what Investors in People is and how it can promote organizational development.

Case Study I
Airedale Springs

The organization

Airedale Springs is a family business founded in 1945. Situated in Haworth, West Yorkshire it employs 68 people in the manufacture of springs, wire forms and light pressings and also offers a design service.

The company is committed to quality both for the product and customer service. It has held ISO 9000 (or its predecessor BS5750) since 1984. It employs modern techniques which enable it to provide a flexible service for small batch and one-off orders as well as for larger quantities.

Reasons for making the initial commitment

The company has always been committed to ensuring the work-force has the skills to deliver the quality product but it had been somewhat ad hoc. The Chairman, Michael Parkinson, was a member of the National Task Force sub-group for Investors in People and was therefore involved in the development of the Standard. He felt the company should go forward for recognition especially as he felt that it would 'have little trouble getting it as it was what they were doing anyway'. He admitted he and his colleagues were in for a shock.

The approach

In September 1991 the company made the formal commitment to start the process of becoming recognized as an Investor in People. They started by carrying out a diagnostic survey of their employees. As a small family concern in a close-knit rural setting it was assumed that all employees understood the business and their role within it. The results of the survey showed there was a complete mismatch between the perception of the owners, the managers and the shop floor. The shop-floor workers felt that management was too secretive and communications were non-existent. Following a review of the findings it was decided that what was needed was a complete culture change to break down the perceived barriers.

As lack of communication was identified as the main problem, a meetings structure was established. Managers would meet weekly and messages would be cascaded from these meetings via a team briefing process to the whole workforce. Simple performance measures were developed and displayed on noticeboards; a news-letter was published with information on projects, events and employee achievements. In addition every six months company briefings were introduced, which all employees were to attend.

It was also felt that aspirations needed to be raised so a merit appraisal review process was introduced. Every six months all employees have a review with their team leader to discuss their potential in relation to predetermined assessment criteria. This assessment may account for up to 30 per cent of an individual's total remuneration. Before meeting their team leader the employees are required to assess themselves, or a team may undertake a team assessment. The appraisal will also include a discussion about personal aspirations, training etc and produces a plan/report, which highlights future training and development actions for the next six months. All employees have personal training files, which are held centrally but are available for each employee on request.

The outcomes from the reviews were that people became more involved in the business. Training activity increased, jobs were twinned which enabled people to have an insight into other people's roles and NVQs were introduced.

The benefits

Michael Parkinson has gone on record as saying that Investors in People saved the company. Twelve months into the implementation process the company was hit by the recession. The open communications and the changing culture meant that the owners were able to discuss the situation and the options with the workforce. Costs needed to be reduced and it was decided that there were two real options: redundancies or a pay cut. The options were put to the workforce who decided to accept the pay cut. During the following six months work picked up and the company weathered the storm. Without the improved communications and trust developed through Investors in People, Michael Parkinson is convinced that the company could well have gone under.

Morale, motivation and job satisfaction have increased throughout the workforce to such an extent that it is noticed by visitors to the company. The changed culture also contributed to the relatively trouble-free introduction of multi-skilling.

There were individual success stories too. A labourer offered training as a skilled operator became a totally different employee when the company found a way to harness his potential through NVQs. He now heads up a new operation and contributes ideas on how to run the business. The first assessment took place in October 1993 when the assessor was satisfied that the company met the Standard and they were subsequently recognized as an Investor In People.

The approach to maintaining the Standard

Since the first assessment many of the processes have been tweaked a little but have continued to run. The take-up of NVQs has increased to such an extent that over 40 per cent of the workforce either have or are taking high level ones. In addition 48 people (out of a total workforce of 68) are now qualified instructors and it is felt that training and development is now part of the culture, which has enabled people to keep fresh. The introduction of new technology always included the appropriate training. The relationship between employees and employer has developed into a partnership, 'a commitment from the employees and a commitment to the employees'.

Reasons for continuing to seek recognition

As long as there are sound business reasons the company will continue to go forward for reassessment. So far the feedback at the end of the assessment from the assessor – a person with an external perspective and with no vested interest – has been extremely beneficial.

Being recognized as an Investor in People has some benefits in relation to customer perception but it is difficult to assess the extent. In the early days of Investors in People, pressure and assistance through the supply chain was thought to be a great incentive to become recognized. Now Michael Parkinson feels the reverse is true and that large companies could learn a lot from small ones. Airedale Springs was re-recognized as an Investor in People in 1996 and is due for a third assessment in 1999.

Case Study II
Barnsley Community and
Priority Services NHS Trust

The organization

In 1985 Barnsley Health Authority created two individual providers of health care – Barnsley District General Hospital and Barnsley Community and Priority Services Unit. In 1992 the unit was given trust status and became Barnsley Community and Priority Services NHS Trust as part of the second wave of NHS trusts.

The Trust provides in-patient and community-based services for all age groups in Barnsley but particularly for children, the elderly, mentally ill people and those with learning disabilities and physically disabled people. The services are provided on five main sites (hospitals and residential units) in Barnsley and from 21 health centres, clinics and a range of other premises throughout the district.

The statutory responsibility for the management of the Trust rests with the Trust board and its directors. The Trust employs 1,600 people who work a complex range of working hours and rotas; a large number are part time. It operates from a relatively flat structure with key service managers reporting directly to the chief executive.

The Trust has a strong emphasis on quality. In 1994 it became the first NHS body to attain ISO 9000 throughout its services. It used this quality system to implement a Continuous Health Improvement Programme (CHIP) which directs the whole organization towards improving services to patients and customers by adapting the principles of total quality management. In 1995 the Trust obtained the charter mark for all its services. A focus on service audits relating to charter issues is used to continually evaluate performance against the rights and standards identified within existing and future patient charters. The Trust is also committed to using the business excellence model as a framework for continual improvement of its services.

Reasons for making the initial commitment

The chief executive made the commitment to Investors in People in March 1995. He felt that the Standard offered a disciplined structure, it ensured that training and development was focused on need and ensured that it evaluated effectiveness. It also linked with the development of a number of other issues such the introduction of appraisals and ISO 9000.

The approach

The chief executive had spent some time working in hospitals in the United States. When the Trust was established, his previous experience of managing a private sector hospital meant he was well placed to manage an NHS trust. For example, he was used to managing budgets, achieving quality and maintaining a spirit of seeking continuous improvement. He was also fortunate in having an active board of directors who supported him.

Communications with the employees was enhanced by the introduction of a team briefing system. An annual communications survey was introduced and established together with an Excellence in Communications team to tackle the problems identified in the survey. A five-year strategic plan, including a mission and quality statement, was developed together with the identification of key success measures. In addition the various services developed three-year business improvement plans. The strategic aim of improving the quality of patient care was publicized in a variety of ways.

Among the key success measures for the human resources department was an 80 per cent take-up of the performance review system which had been introduced to replace the previous appraisal system that operated sporadically throughout the organization. The new scheme allowed the option of either individual or team review. The idea of team reviews was necessary as some managers had up to 40 people reporting to them. As well as the review everyone had the right to ask for a personal development plan. For qualified nurses this is important, as they have to demonstrate continuous professional development in the form of post-registration education and practice (PREP) in order to maintain their nursing registration.

Management development

The Trust recognized that management development and in partic-ular the management of people was critical to the success of its plans. It undertook a number of steps to ensure its managers were competent to take on these responsibilities. A large number attended a first line managers' course, which was supported by other modules; for example all managers who carry out performance reviews have to undergo appropriate training. The Trust also supported the achievement of appropriate external qualifications with a number having the English National Board 997/998 Clinical Teaching and Assessment certificates and a number have also obtained management NVQs. Senior staff were also encouraged to attend the Managing Health Services course and two senior managers undertook a diploma in management course run in partnership with the TEC and various local industries. The Trust also established a learning resource centre to support training and development.

Evaluation

The quest for value for money for any expenditure was driven by the board; training and development expenditure was not an excep-tion. Each month the human resources department presented to the board a report on progress towards the executive objectives. An annual report against the key success measures is also presented and as part of this report the human resources department collates a cost-benefit analysis of training and development based on reports from department managers.

At the team and individual level the Trust evaluates the effective-ness of training through a variety of methods, eg end-of-course critiques, tests, quizzes and through the performance reviews, etc. The whole process of evaluation is included and audited through the ISO procedures. In September 1996 the Trust came forward for assessment and was recognized as an Investor in People.

The benefits

One of the reasons for introducing Investors in People was to focus the training on needs. This happened to such an extent in one area of the Trust that some people felt that Investors had reduced their access to training. Prior to Investors in People being introduced they had had unlimited access to training but under Investors they had to justify training in terms of meeting the needs of the Trust, which they were not always able to do. However, other people were getting more training. Investors in People was seen to be an import-ant step along the continuous improvement route and it established a firm foundation in the Trust's organizational development strategy.

Since being recognized

Since being recognized the Trust has continued to train and develop staff and assess the benefits but it has also placed an emphasis on reviewing and improving its processes. In 1998 part of the Trust, the Kendray Hospital, attained Nurse Development Unit status which recognizes it as a centre of excellent practice development. In 1999 the Trust was re-awarded the charter mark in recognition of its excellent services.

The concept of clinical governance has recently been introduced by the Government in its White Paper, 'The New NHS: Modern and Dependable'. This lays a duty on trusts to ensure that profes-sional staff are continuously developed to guarantee best working practice. Investors in People recognition together with other quality initiatives contribute to attracting and retaining the high calibre of staff who work for the Barnsley Community and Priority Services NHS Trust.

Case Study III
Bidwells

The company

Bidwells is a legal partnership[1] specializing in property services to the rural, commercial and residential markets in the east of England and in Scotland. It was founded around 1840 in Ely by Charles Bidwell. It is a multi-discipline partnership of property consultants, valuers, project managers and agents employing 325 people in locations at Cambridge, Ipswich, Northampton, Bury St Edmunds, London, Perth and Inverness.

Growth during the 1980s and 1990s included consolidation of Bidwells' traditional role and expansion into new areas based on long-term potential for commercial development and management (eg a science park, docks). The firm's financial performance in 1996 exceeded budget and did so again in 1997. Turnover stands at £11 million split between rural activities (£5.5m), commercial (£4.5m) and residential (£1m). The main activities include:

- *Rural:* estate management and planning, estate and farm accounting services, farm business tenancies, etc.
- *Commercial:* property management, valuation planning applications, etc.
- *Residential:* purchase and sale of large country houses, inspections and surveys, lettings, etc.
- *Building and design services:* concept, design, planning, fitting, etc.
- *Drawing:* maps, charts, site plans, etc.

Why Investors in People?

Bidwells made a formal commitment in March 1994 to Cambridge-shire TEC to work towards becoming an Investor in People organization. It undertook Investors in People to support the considerable organizational change it was undergoing.

Bidwells was successfully recognized in October 1997 and, having opted for the 12–15-month developmental review reassessment, retained the Standard in October 1998. Demonstrably confident of its continued success in embedding cultural change it is looking forward to the next 12–15-month developmental review in November 1999.

Commitment

The managing partner demonstrates commitment in many ways: his meetings with staff, the restructuring exercise consultative process and notably the electronic bulletin board that staff must access to get into their PC. The Bidwells mission is, 'To be nationally recognized as the foremost firm of property consultants in the Eastern Region.' To help employees at all levels understand their role, this statement is accompanied by an explanation of the thinking behind it. Business plan review exercises offered further opportunities for awareness, understanding and interpretation of the vision.

The managing partner summarized the current – and very different – approach to restructuring as compared to nine years ago, 'It was a doddle; we only asked nine people! This time we are rightly seeing it as a major undertaking with everyone being consulted. It's much, much better.' Divisions have their own plans, which start off with the overall plan as a base and flesh out the salient elements.

Drawn from the overall business plan, each division produces its own training plan within its own business plan. There are two main thrusts. First, there are initiatives that derive from the business plan itself delivered via the central budget. Second, there are those that emanate from the appraisal.

Appraisal and review

All posts are revised and reviewed on a regular basis via appraisal and at entry. The appraisal process is the key vehicle. All staff have an appraisal during which their training and development needs are considered. The appraisal process offers a flexible methodology with the same aims. It is not a 'once a year process'; there are formal and informal mini reviews taking place at other times during the planning cycle. The value of the process for Bidwells is the opportunity for an in-depth conversation about work, the working environment and professional development. To that end the process made allowance for different styles. Every effort is made to ensure the process was 'bespoke' to the particular member of staff, while seeking to meet the same objectives.

At the *organizational* level, staff training and development needs are regularly discussed at divisional board meetings. Priorities are refined in line with business objectives at these and other meetings. The managing partner is not only internally appraised but also participates in a network with other senior professionals in the area. At the team and individual levels, office meetings, sector and divisional meetings review and revise as appropriate. Professional staff and trainees have to demonstrate continuous professional development (CPD) on a continuous basis to external bodies (Royal Institute of Chartered Surveyors etc). These are monitored and reviewed internally. Professional staff are reviewed against 'chargeable time' and CPD which is externally benchmarked and internally monitored.

The managing partner conducts mini reviews at various stages during the operating cycle and is himself subjected to review and appraisal by the main board (comprising the equity partners). There is also an element of upward appraisal for the managing partner via presentation and discussion sessions on progress against targets made annually to the divisional managing partners and their senior colleagues.

Objectives and objective setting

Training and development is linked to business objectives (via business/training plans) and incorporates individually expressed needs as appropriate (via appraisal, where objectives are set at the individual level). Divisional reviews are the principal vehicle for agreeing the broader business objectives. All divisions produce a training and development plan framed within the parameters of the organizational business plan.

The appraisal process includes the following objectives:

- to praise and give thanks;
- to recognize good work, encourage and motivate;
- to discuss difficulties with work or with relationships;
- to look forward to the year ahead and discuss work issues;
- (in the case of professional staff) to see evidence of CPD and to initial the record;
- to make provision for any necessary training, experience or other development.

A particular success was the 'mystery shopper' programme. Here, in line with organizational improvement objectives, an initial study was carried out to examine the firm's ability to respond appropriately when dealing with random callers. The information from this study was used to set up a range of activities relating to improving skills in recognizing business opportunities during a telephone conversation.

Induction

The comprehensive induction process is essentially employee led but has inputs from human resources and others at the local level as appropriate. There are checks and balances to ensure completion such as a checklist which, if not returned, will be 'chased up' by the human resources department. The induction for graduate trainees is in addition to this and takes place formally for a week in September each year, the time of recruitment.

Evaluation

With regard to knowledge, one example was again the 'mystery shopper' study and the resultant training and development actions in improving effectiveness. Skill areas outside the 'normal' professional remit such as IT or marketing are evaluated in terms of impact; for example, course critiques, opinion surveys, an evaluation of one division's marketing training, and the evaluation of a business writing course. Taking a broader view, Bidwells has been constantly striving to engender an attitude change over the past decade, moving away from the more traditional, conservative, autocratic form of organizational structure to a more 'people first' orientation. The Investors in People process has supported this especially with regard to the training and development of the support staff. The introduction – and acceptance, use and perceived value – of the appraisal process is an excellent example of measuring the impact of training and development on attitudes.

The business plan states that:

> In order to increase productivity, motivation and job satisfaction we are committed to improving the qualities of leadership, departmental responsibility and co-operation among all staff. This will be achieved through training, accelerated experience and increased devolution of management. Where new staff are recruited, the ability to play a team role will be an important factor.

In spite of tight cost control in all areas, the investment in training and development has increased over the past few years as evident improvements have been noted and acted upon (eg actual income greater than projected for 1998 and similar expected for 1999). This increase in investment is evidenced in several ways:

- the direct increase in the specific training and development budget;
- the mini reviews against the targets that the managing partner conducts on a regular basis;
- the business plan review consultation process;
- the 'justification' by the head of human resources to the partners and the divisions of the costs they have to support;
- the divisions' own evident understanding of the benefits (eg increased revenue from 'chargeable time').

Evaluation takes place at several levels and can be described as continuous. In the main, evaluation takes place in a 'culturally appropriate way'. In essence this means that feedback is actively sought from clients via such strategies as client satisfaction questionnaires, one-to-one discussions, indirect feedback, senior staff intervention at key stages (informal or formal) and, notably, via 'networks' that professional staff actively belong to.

Key benefits

- The process gives emphasis and focus to 'people processes'.
- Bidwells was able to install systems and procedures that contributed to the achievement of the business plan.
- The culture change away from 'an autocratic, top-down, benevolent paternalism and towards a modern commercial enterprise' could not have been achieved without the discipline of Investors in People.
- It has provided a framework within which individuals have grown and taken ownership of their part of the business, thinking their own way through the challenges of genuine growth. Communicating policy, seeking commitment through consultation, publicizing successes – all have built up the cumulative effect.

Key message

The main board's public commitment to business objectives has been reinforced by appropriate resources and is accompanied by a determination to carry people forward. Bidwells has now become an organization determined 'to make the best use of its people, stretching them to new achievements'.

Note

1. A legal partnership's structure can be complex. In essence, Bidwells has a structure comprising three sectors (commercial, rural and residential) and seven divisions. Each sector has a co-ordinator who is an equity partner. Four divisions are geographical and are therefore multi-disciplinary in nature. Three are product divisions. As a legal partnership the structure is described in terms of reporting relationships. These, beginning

with the managing partner, relate to the divisions and sectors described above. The senior staff are the equity partners who have sectoral and divisional responsibilities in addition to their professional role, one of whom is elected by the main board (the equity partners) to act as managing partner. The next tier, as it were, is associate partners. All assume a range of divisional management responsibilities in addition to their professional role within the rural, commercial or residential sectors.

Case Study IV
Brodeur A Plus

The company

Brodeur A Plus (formerly the A Plus Group) is a marketing and communications consultancy specializing in companies primarily in the information technology sector. In the UK, it currently employs some 80 people. This number is expected to continue to increase as the company successfully implements its strategy to be the world's first global high technology marketing communications firm.

The company was established in the UK in 1981 since when it has consistently achieved year-on-year revenue growth of 20 per cent. This growth has been fuelled by a strategy that has attracted to its client base some of the world's largest firms – GE, IBM, Nortel Networks, Philips and Siemens, for instance. As part of its vision of building a global firm, in the early 1990s, the then A Plus Group developed Euro Plus, a network of affiliates that worked throughout the United States, Europe, the Middle East and Africa. The need to consolidate this activity, to bring it under a common brand and the desire to expand the company into the Pacific Rim and South America resulted, early in 1997, in the directors of the A Plus Group selling the company into the ownership of Omnicom, one of the world's largest media groups. Omnicom, which had already acquired A Plus Group's US affiliate, Brodeur and Partners, would provide the backing both for the acquisition of existing affiliates and the establishment of affiliates and wholly owned offices in South America, the Far East and the Pacific Rim. 1998 has seen the establishment of regional headquarters in Boston,

Miami, Singapore and Slough, the acquisition of partners in Europe and the establishment of affiliate networks throughout the Pacific Rim and South America. In total, the Brodeur organization now involves over 650 people worldwide.

As the A Plus Group, Brodeur A Plus was one of the first 28 companies to be recognized as an Investor in People, in October 1991. It retained this recognition when the company was reassessed successfully both in 1994 and 1997.

Why Investors in People?

Since its founding Brodeur A Plus had nurtured a culture of investing in people as a primary engine for business growth. When Investors in People was established in 1991 the company examined the concept immediately. Brodeur A Plus found that the framework offered by Investors in People coincided with the company overhauling its human resources practices and management structures in preparation for further growth. From this point, Investors in People offered the ongoing discipline that the company desired if it was to achieve its business targets.

In particular, the company needed to push decision making down the organization, as far as possible requiring people to think and act as defined by best practice, a process that has continued to this day. This led to an ongoing skills development and personnel management programme to equip employees at all levels to meet these requirements.

The benefits

In 1991 the company was quoted as saying that participation in Investors in People brought focus to 'a more efficient, planned recruitment and development process, a more structured team approach as well as improved management skills in line with business needs'. So when the third anniversary of the Investors in People accreditation approached and reassessment against the Standard was required, the company 'never considered not being reassessed', an attitude which has pervaded it to this day and through a subsequent reassessment.

Prior to its first reassessment the company took stock of its processes. Although a great deal of training and development had taken place it had lost the focus on recording and evaluating the development; other priorities had got in the way. The need for reassessment therefore brought this to its attention and in the time available it was able to put this element of managing the development back at the centre of the agenda and has continued to do so ever since.

Current activity

Through two reassessments the company has gone from strength to strength with the search for quality through continual improvement being a key theme. Early in 1995, the Odyssey Project was launched. This five-year plan has involved further structural change in order that the directors should be able to devote less time to mainstream account handling and more time to managing a dynamic business, both in the UK and Europe. It has also involved group account directors having a greater responsibility for running the business on a day-to-day basis and managing the development of people. As the company has grown and the need to manage international business too has increased, the company has been divided into self-managing business units. These units have discrete employees and client bases, each headed by a business group director, most of whom have been developed from Brodeur A Plus's original cadre of group account directors.

These changes have been underpinned by the development of what Brodeur A Plus considers to be the most advanced development environment in the PR industry. This is centred around the professional excellence programme (PEP), a modular programme in six stages linked to the development needs of different executive levels within the organization. It was developed to Brodeur A Plus's specification initially involving an external contractor. It is competency-based, with exercises assessed by line managers and Brodeur A Plus's people development director. The programme is reassessed continually and refined. All executive staff are required to go through the PEP programme as a prerequisite to promotion, as are graduate administrative staff. PEP is linked to a comprehensive induction, coaching and training programme with modules designed specifically to support PEP that allow individuals to achieve rapid advancement through the company in support of international expansion. The company has introduced a series of international training modules, conducted with other companies in the Brodeur Europe organization and these too are linked to PEP.

As part of fulfilling its mission to be the 'first choice consultancy for global IT companies', Brodeur A Plus has developed a European and European/US Staff Exchange Programme (STEP/STEP-UP) which involves Brodeur A Plus staff working in affiliate offices in continental Europe, Scandinavia and the United States.

The need for continuous improvement

As a specialist in the marketing of information technology, the company considers itself to be at the 'fast end of the fastest moving industry sector'. Brodeur A Plus needs to look constantly for improvements through formal and informal client feedback, benchmarking and learning through the job. For example, each executive is equipped with a custom training needs analysis which is revised formally at twice-yearly appraisals and informally as new challenges are met.

A customer service charter has been developed as part of a quality programme. As part of this process, clients are required to complete questionnaires and take part in feedback interviews with Brodeur A Plus's managing director twice a year, with additional assessment by independent consultants once a year. The company also surveys its own staff twice a year, a process managed by the company's recently formed management forum – a group of account managers and directors. The results from each type of survey are actively fed back into development planning.

With all this activity taking place, Brodeur A Plus is confident that when reassessment comes around again in 2000 it will be well placed to retain its status as an Investor in People. In addition, it is now meeting the challenge of implementing Investors in People globally. The company has been chosen by Investors in People UK to be one of the first international pilots for Investors in People and is currently working to implement the Standard in its Boston office.

Case Study V
Queen Elizabeth's Boys School

The organization

Queen Elizabeth's Boys School was established in 1573 and has been a fully functional school for over 400 years. The original site of the school was in Wood Street, Barnet and it moved during the 1930s to larger premises at its current location in Queen's Road, Barnet. The school provides for some 1,150 pupils in the age range of 12 to 18.

A former grant-maintained school, Queen Elizabeth's Boys School is now a foundation school. Legal responsibility for the school lies with the governing body, while responsibility for the daily management of the school lies with the headmaster.

There is a senior management team comprising 10 senior staff who act as coaching leaders to the 70+ full-time teachers who make up the teaching staff. There are some 30 support staff who work for the school in administrative, cleaning, catering or site/buildings capacities. The school is heavily oversubscribed and is ranked by Ofsted as being among the top 10 per cent of maintained schools in the public examination league tables. The section on benefits below draws, appropriately, on the Ofsted report. In addition the school has a strong tradition of achievements in sport and music. The school mission is to produce boys who are 'confident, able and responsible'.

Evaluation of training and development

The school has a record of staff training providing a catalogue of all training undertaken since 1989 (the year it went grant maintained). The investment in training and development is controlled by the senior tutor who ensures that suggested development activities are in line with agreed targets and priorities. One of the clearest measures of performance improvement as an outcome of investment in training and development is the school's examination results. These have improved markedly since 1989. The school is now in the top 10 maintained boys schools as well as being in the top 10 comprehensives in the country.

The school has a clear training plan; skills gaps are identified and measures are taken to close these gaps. The channel for these measures is the TKON system (see below) and currently the termly review with support staff. The TKON system is the measure used by the organization to evaluate its development actions. The headmaster is 'the anchor' of the system and all reports go to him. This is followed by analysis and further recommendations at cabinet, the senior staff team meeting.

Appraisal

TKON is the school's own organizational target-setting and review mechanism, comprising individual and group meetings with staff based upon individual contribution to the school's mission. Goals are set, progressed and assessed in terms of the mission. Although the system originally related to academic staff only, following review of the current system for support staff, and as part of its commitment to continuous improvement, the school is establishing this as the system for all staff. The term is therefore not an acronym, rather it is part of the language 'currency' of the school.

Objectives

An example demonstrating that development actions had achieved their objectives can be seen in the school's IT strategy. The objective was to improve efficiency via the introduction of the SIMS communication software. The school now holds a SIMS site of excellence certificate and joins a small group of schools who have achieved this level of performance with the administrative software.

Training outcomes for individuals are assessed at TKON level and at department level. The senior tutor acts as a monitor of all training applications and related expenditure; these applications have also to be endorsed by the department or subject heads and by the deputy head responsible for staffing. Examination results and applications for places are the key organizational level indicators. The boys themselves were seen by staff as an excellent indicator as to the effectiveness of their own training and development.

The governing body regularly receives reports on the costs and benefits of the development process. The senior tutor is a regular guest at governors' meetings (as are most other senior staff and cabinet members). The headmaster has a formal target-setting meeting with the chair of the governors and regular reviews are held throughout the year. Proposals and costings of training are a matter of regular discussion. Managers are now expected to draft departmental development plans which enhance performance in relation to the school's mission. The first question on the staff development programme application forms asks how the programme relates to the school mission.

The principal performance criteria (exam results, applications, the annual record of achievement and the size of the sixth form) are systematically relayed to staff through a variety of measures, both formal and informal. Formally, this is done through the weekly briefing (written and verbal), TKON/departmental follow-ups and governors' meetings (there are two staff governors and it is custom and practice for other staff to sit in on meetings).

The benefits

There have been many external benefits, notably the National Training Award and resulting Supreme Winner status and the acquisition of a grant from the National Grid for Learning (which contributed significantly to IT development). Overall, the benefits of Investors in People can, in the opinion of the school, best be summed up by the Ofsted report, elements of which are quoted below:

- The school meets its mission of producing young men who are confident, able and responsible.
- The school is successful in helping boys reach high standards of achievement in all areas of their lives.
- This is a harmonious school. The pupils are good listeners and respect the views of others. Boys from different backgrounds work well together and learn from each other's beliefs. Pupils feel safe in sharing personal experiences and beliefs, and are not afraid to be challenged or challenge others as constructive arguments take place in a respectful and tolerant environment.
- Pupils and staff value each other and feel valued.
- An outstanding feature is the very high standard of teaching which produces exceptional public examination results – compared with other schools, overall standards of teaching in all subjects are most often outstanding.
- Classroom management is of a very high standard.
- Behaviour in all areas of the school is excellent.
- Target setting to help future improvement of work is developing very well.
- The attitude of the boys is of an excellent standard.
- Behaviour in all areas of the school is excellent.
- The provision for social development is excellent.
- Work experience is well supported by excellent careers education.

Case Study VI
Raflatac Limited

The organization

Raflatac Limited produces self-adhesive label stock for the labelling industry. It is Finnish owned, part of the United Paper Mills-Kymmene Corporation, the third largest forest industry group in the world. Raflatac is the market leader in the UK and much of Europe and is expanding into new and growing markets throughout the world.

Raflatac Limited consists of three sites: the manufacturing site in Scarborough and two distribution sites in Stevenage and Dublin. It employs just under 300 people in total at the three locations.

The site at Scarborough opened in 1975. In 1989 the company became aware of the management philosophy of Deming, the US statistician, which it hoped would bring about a radical change in thinking and attitudes. Following his philosophy it introduced and developed its own approach to continuous improvement, which has lead to improvements in both the perception of its customers and the morale of its staff.

The commitment to Investors in People

During 1991 the company became aware of the Investors in People Standard and realized much of what it was doing was already taking it towards the Standard. In March 1992 it made the commitment to work towards the Investors in People Standard which it felt would ensure it maintained or improved upon what it was already doing. In December 1992 it was recognized as an Investor in People. In addition to being recognized as an Investor in People the company achieved BS ISO 9002 and its commitment to protecting the environment and conserving energy resulted in achieving ISO 14000.

Maintaining the Standard

Since 1992 the company has been successfully reassessed twice. There are two main reasons why it has continued to retain its recognition as an Investor in People. First it is proud of the achievement and doesn't want to lose it. Second, and perhaps most importantly, it finds it helpful that an independent and impartial person takes a look at its training and development processes. It found the subsequent feedback either reinforced existing plans or gave it further ideas for future development and continuous improvement.

What has it done to maintain recognition?

The company's philosophy is (and always has been) one of involving all employees and it regards itself as a team. This was demonstrated by an event in 1995, organized by the management board of the company, which brought all its employees (including those working in Dublin and Stevenage) together. The event involved a review of the company's history and future plans, the views of the MD and of one of its customers and ended with a 'Question Time' event chaired by an external facilitator with members of the board forming the panel. There are plans to repeat this event in 1999.

In order to improve communication it has introduced monthly team briefing, developed an internal Intranet and given all employees an e-mail address. Employees can access both the e-mail and the Intranet through PCs that are located throughout the sites. They can also access e-mails from the head office in Finland and the global Intranet.

The company demonstrates its commitment to training and developing employees in a variety of ways. It has continued to train all employees in the tools and techniques to identify and implement continuous improvement initiatives. Training manuals and checklists have been rewritten and on-the-job trainers have been trained. An open learning centre is being developed and in response to feedback from new starters the recruitment and induction process has been improved. This was carried out by a group of recent inductees who were formed into an improvement group. Customer visits and work shadowing has been encouraged.

Raflatac Limited offers three levels of study support for training and education that lead to qualifications. For qualifications directly relevant to their current job, employees are given financial support, time and travelling expenses incurred. For qualifications which are not directly relevant to their current job but may be relevant in the future, fees are paid but study must be carried out in the employee's own time. The third level has no strict criteria other than that it should involve structured learning. The level of support is £75 per employee per year. A variety of activities have been supported, ranging from golf and driving lessons to computing skills. The company has also continued to work closely with the community and with young people through an education business partnership.

In the quest for the right mixture of management styles it initially introduced its managers to the Dale Carnegie philosophies. The company recently learnt about the work of Dr Steven Covey and felt that by attending workshops developed by Covey it would fill a gap between Deming and Dale Carnegie. It is still early days but it is felt that these workshops have changed people.

The performance of the company is monitored through a number of key performance factors (KPFs). Through this monitoring it can be demonstrated how training and development activities contribute to efficiencies that have been achieved. For example, over a period of time, lead-in times have been reduced, machine speeds have been increased, waste reduced and quality improved. Future plans focus on further improvement in performance especially in the area of reducing costs as the possibility of a recession looms. The principles that underpin Investors in People will continue to play a significant part in these plans.

Case Study VII
Renaissance London
Heathrow Hotel

The organization

The Renaissance London Heathrow Hotel (formerly the Ramada Hotel) is one of four Renaissance Hotels in the UK, the others being at Gatwick, Manchester and Reading. It is part of the Renaissance Hotel Group owned by Marriott Lodging International, which has hotels worldwide. This hotel has 650 bedrooms and employs 280 staff. Marriott took over its management in April 1997.

The group of hotels (then Ramada Hotels) originally became interested in Investors in People in early 1994 and undertook a diagnostic exercise in June of that year. The diagnosis showed that the hotels had quite different structures and were likely to go forward at different rates. They decided therefore to work towards the Investors in People Standard independently, although they liaised with one another throughout the process.

Reasons for making the initial commitment

The timing of the original commitment coincided with a previous change of ownership (it was then the Heathrow Penta) and there was an urgent need to change the culture, introduce flexible working practices and encourage staff to become more involved. Investors in People was seen as the tool to help this come about.

It also displayed:

- a black-and-white commitment to looking after staff;
- a commitment to both guests and customers;
- a number of PR benefits which were expected as an end result.

The approach

Feeling that they did not want to pay lip service to the process, the approach adopted by the hotel had been to include all heads of department from the start. This involved the heads meeting to learn what Investors in People was all about, seeking their commitment, and brainstorming ideas about the way forward.

They decided to produce action plans department by department. These have been produced by involving all staff in the planning process. The action plans are based on the answers to three questions:

- Where are we now?
- Where do we want to be?
- How will we get there?

This approach and the use of the three questions has continued to be a cornerstone of the approach to maintaining the Standard. Throughout the process the general manager of the hotel has been also thoroughly involved. During the early stages at each weekly management meeting a head of department was invited to report progress.

The human resources department saw its job as facilitating the process, which was and continues to be led and owned by heads of department. Action plans are devised and examined and these have led to a range of training and development activities, with an enormous number of ideas for improvements to the service offered to customers, all of them generated by employees. The department looks for areas where needs are common and meets those needs on a hotel-wide basis. Among these, prioritizing, statutory and mandatory issues, customer care, management development, core skills, computer literacy and on-the-job training have become focal points.

The hotel created a training room as an immediate benefit. Almost immediately there was a definite buzz about the place. Investors posters were displayed throughout the hotel to keep the subject in people's minds. Everybody got involved and took the opportunity to contribute towards Investors in People. They have had a lot of help, particularly in the form of workshops from West London TEC.

Initially the main issues that the hotel faced concerned managing the varying degrees of enthusiasm and commitment from the heads of department. This enthusiasm led to one department leaping forward so fast that the others were somewhat left behind. Asking their department to hold back may have affected their enthusiasm but did not lead to a lessening of commitment. Gradually all the other departments caught up.

However, in July 1995 some doubts started to emerge whether the target date of September 1995 for assessment would be met. It was decided to rerun the original survey, similar to the one in Appendix 2 of this book. The survey results indicated that the hotel met the requirements of the Standard but it was the replies to an additional question that was asked that really convinced the general manager that the hotel was ready for assessment. The additional question and the responses are shown in Table VII.1.

Table VII.1 *What is your most common feeling at the end of a working shift or day?*

Glad to go home	21%
Frustrated	4%
Satisfied and appreciated	16%
Looking forward to tomorrow	11%
Wish for better things	8%
Proud to have done something worthwhile	40%

Needless to say, when the assessment took place in September 1995 the staff satisfied the assessor that the hotel met the Standard and they were subsequently recognized as an Investor In People.

Reasons for continuing to seek recognition

The change of ownership to Marriott coincided with the run-up to the reassessment. Investors in People was again seen as the ideal vehicle to help manage the changes. The hotel had gained lots of benefits from the recognition as an Investor in People. These had included PR benefits and financial benefits in the form of increased revenue and profit every year since 1994. However, most important has been people benefits. The original 'buzz' had been retained; staff were proud to wear their lapel badges displaying the Investors logo. The friendliness, efficiency and commitment of staff had been important in contributing to the hotel receiving many accolades such as Conference Hotel of Year in 1995/1996/1997 and Best Conference Venue 1998/99 from *Business Travel Magazine*. Feedback from guests and visitors showed that the hotel was highly thought of. The general manager did not want to risk losing all of this by allowing the recognition to slip.

It had also been noticeable that, during the uncertain period of 16 months following the takeover by Marriott, staff turnover remained low. The hotel general manager believes that the feeling of belonging implanted by Investors in People contributed significantly to this low turnover.

The approach to maintaining the Standard

Many of the changes were significant; for example, the new owners operated on a different financial year. They had their own corporate standards, which meant all staff had to undergo an induction to the new organization. The senior organizational changes at the Renaissance Hotel Group's Regional head office level when Marriott took over caused a delay in the delivery of this corporate induction so in the meantime the Heathrow Hotel continued with its programme of internal training to ensure that business objectives were achieved.

Many of the original processes were retained. The strong culture of communicating to and involving staff continued. The training of in-house trainers was further developed so that on-the-job training was further developed. The commitment of management to training and developing staff has continued to play an important part.

Benefits to staff

Not only has the hotel as a whole benefited significantly from Investors in People, the staff have too. During the three years between assessments 48 staff were promoted to higher positions, 29 of whom were promoted to other hotels within the company. In December 1998, in recognition of the work he had done in promoting Investors in People, the general manager was given a Key Crusader Award by Investors in People UK. In September 1998 the hotel was reassessed and again the assessor was satisfied that the hotel had continued to meet the requirements of the Investors in People Standard.

Case Study VIII
University of Sunderland

The University of Sunderland committed to Investors in People in January 1993. It was first recognized in February 1996 and was subsequently re-recognized in March 1999.

The organization

The University of Sunderland has around 15,000 students and 1,800 staff. It has six schools and 22 service departments all based within the city but on three campuses. An ex-polytechnic, it became a university in 1992. It was awarded the charter mark, again on a whole institution basis, in 1997.

The early 1990s saw a period of major change for the institution including a significant restructuring, a doubling of student numbers, the building of a new campus and becoming a university. The institution had ambitious plans and a determination to succeed. It recognized that the main route to success lay through its people, ie the performance of its staff. It needed a professional and planned approach to staff development in order to align staff behind the goals of the institution and to enable people to maximize their performance.

The first assessment

Interest first began with the university appointing a staff development manager and, later, an Investors in People 'champion' – David Williams – in September 1992. The university then allocated significant resources for staff development, and in January 1993 made a formal public commitment to achieving the Investors in People National Standard within three years. It was felt that Investors in People provided a template for professional practice. Investors in People also provided motivation for management, a means to measure progress during the course of these three years, and ultimately an external assurance of the quality of what the university was doing.

The staff development manager's job was to pursue a professional and quality staff development service as well as to project-manage achievement of the Investors in People Standard. These two activities ran in parallel alongside each other, slowly converging as the Investors in People assessment approached. The intention was that the university would – through gaining Investors in People recognition – have 'reached a sufficient level of best practice so that Investors in People could then drop off the visible agenda'.

When the university first achieved Investors in People status in 1996 it felt that those two parallel 'lines' had indeed converged: 'We had a staff development policy, a staff development strategy, annual staff development plans at individual, departmental and university level, appraisal for all staff etc. Not until we matured further as an organization did we realize that this was not the case: the "lines" were still some way apart!' Much more work was needed, particularly in the area of evaluation, in order truly to achieve best practice.

Reassessment

The university says that it collectively needed to work very much harder in order to prepare for – and succeed at – re-recognition in 1999. Importantly, the university notes that this was:

> not that the Standard had become harder to achieve, nor that we had let our standards drop, but because we now had a greater understanding of what constituted best practice in staff development within higher education and, to a certain extent, we had raised our expectations of what was achievable and desirable. Such is the nature of continuous improvement.

The approach

Following the first assessment, the university designed its own diagnostic tool to assess internally the university against the Standard. This tool evolved over the years and indeed was adapted again for use in the recent reassessment. Initially it was needed to inform the Investors in People action plan. The tool gave the university a baseline against which to measure progress, a better understanding of where the early emphasis should be, and where resources should be primarily directed. During the three years of the Investors in People project the tool was used at intervals to assess progress. Project Manager David Williams also notes that: 'there is a danger of over-use of a diagnostic tool: even one whose design is regularly changed can become overly "familiar" to staff completing it, which can bias the results'.

Returns of completed questionnaires diminished the more the tool was used. Academic staff may complete a questionnaire once, but few will give it much attention a second or third time, meaning that as the project progressed the university mainly received back completed returns from other staff, resulting in biased samples. It then set up a project team of 'consultants' from the business school whose task it was to provide guidance to departmental managers and to assist local contacts. Their understanding of their allocated departments over time proved useful as a source of informal feedback. This enabled the Investors in People project manager to steer a whole institution forward to assessment, confident that he knew broadly what was going on.

Each of the schools and services nominated staff ('there were even a few volunteers!') to become their Investors in People contact/champion. Their role was:

- to become a conduit for two-way information;
- to be an editor of language, translating the 'business'-like language of Investors in People ('it is much better now, it has to be said') to suit the culture/ethos of their particular department;
- to provide assistance to the Investors in People project manager;
- to identify examples of good practice: to be shared between the champions, and ultimately used by the project manager in compiling the university's portfolio of evidence at assessment;
- to provide diagnosis and analysis.

The university notes how, over time, several of these champions have evolved into staff development 'experts' or at least been given staffing responsibilities in relation to the planning and management of staff development within their department. When they went for reassessment they maintained the champion's role but did not see the necessity any more for a project team. In effect, with time the champions became 'consultants' too.

Key challenges

The main issues identified were:

- the relatively poorly developed role of the line manager/team leader, particularly among academic staff;
- articulating and, particularly, communicating 'business' objectives;
- the alignment of developmental objectives with performance objectives – at all levels but particularly at the individual level;
- evaluation;
- top-level understanding, monitoring and control.

Key messages

- the need to speak two languages: 'one for the assessors who knew very little about higher education, and another for the staff (who knew very little about Investors in People . . .)';
- the need to gain real commitment and co-operation at both the top of the institution and at local level;
- to consider all employees in planning and activity, and not just a select few or those showing interest;
- to consider scholarly activity undertaken by academics as staff development, but remember that if you do so then you will have to ensure that you can show you apply the Investors in People model to this activity!
- do not attempt Investors in People on the cheap: it is not that Investors in People is in itself expensive, but investing in staff development can be;
- consider the resources committed to staff development to be an investment and not a cost;

- develop the means of monitoring and evaluating this investment.

The benefits

The university recognizes that the benefits of pursuing and achieving the Standard are not the awards and accolades that follow, but instead the impact upon university staff, their performance and that of the university in meeting its strategic and operational goals. By utilizing Investors in People the university is better able to align its staff behind the university's objectives while at the same time enabling staff to fulfil their own needs and ambitions.

In a complex organization like a university, it is not possible or desirable to claim a rather simplistic cause and effect. However, the university has no doubt that, by operating the best practice within the Standard, and maintaining the levels of investment in staff development (currently 4 per cent of turnover), there is clearly a relationship with its success in relation to Investors in People.

Within a difficult economic environment for higher education, the University of Sunderland in recent years has nonetheless:

- reduced unit costs by 36% per student during the 1990s;
- doubled its student numbers in a four-year period;
- increased its fee income by 7.2% over 1998–99;
- achieved 'excellent' ratings from Ofsted for its secondary teacher training provision;
- improved both its national rating and its level of funding in the last research assessment exercise;
- shown major improvements in recent teaching quality assessments so that all of its recent exercises have produced the equivalent of 'excellent' scores, indeed culminating in March 1999 in achievement of the maximum possible score for the biosciences teaching quality assessment.

CHAPTER 9

The Kirkpatrick Four-level Model of Evaluation

We are often asked the question 'What is evaluation?' To answer that in the modern context it is appropriate to begin with the Donald Kirkpatrick four-level model of evaluation. This chapter seeks to explore the model that nearly four decades ago revolutionized the thinking of managers, trainers and developers in this area. It is still without a doubt the main and often only approach of which most organizations are aware. Many trainers and developers will say unashamedly that they have yet to find something better or more appropriate to their needs. The longevity of the model is noteworthy, Kirkpatrick's four-level model of evaluation was introduced via four articles in the *Journal for the American Society of Training Directors* between November 1958 and February 1959. (The journal is now called *Training and Development*.) Kirkpatrick is not without his critics (see Chapter 13, The Responsive Organization), but his contribution remains highly significant in a largely underdeveloped area.

The model

In essence, Kirkpatrick sought to stimulate those with responsibility for the management of training and development to increase their efforts in evaluating training and development actions. The model comprises four levels or steps. It is important to note that many commentators use 'level' in this context as being indicative of superiority/inferiority. This is not necessarily the case and was not the intention of Kirkpatrick to establish a hierarchy of evaluation imperatives. Each level shown in Table 9.1 measures different but complementary aspects of a training and development action.

Table 9.1 *Kirkpatrick's four-level model*

Reaction	What the participants felt about the project or programme – the 'happy sheet'
Learning	Internal validation – were the objectives met?
Behaviour	External validation – has training transfer taken place?
Results	Has the project/programme made a difference, ie what has been the impact on the institution?

Step I: Reaction

Kirkpatrick defines this as 'how well trainees like a particular training programme. Evaluating in terms of reaction is the same as measuring trainees' feelings. *It doesn't measure any learning that takes place*' (present authors' emphasis). 'Like' can be interpreted as including such things as venue, catering, organization and administration. All this information is clearly of potential value to those responsible for the delivery of that particular service, provided they receive relevant summary information in an appropriate and useable format.

Reaction is easy to measure and easier to quantify. Therefore nearly all training and development managers employing some form of evaluation use it. It has value and merit, but can so very often be the only methodology employed. If this is the case, any results based on this and this alone will be relatively meaningless, however much the end product is dressed up by complex formulae and presentation styles.

The reaction sheet or 'happy sheet'

A good happy sheet knows what it wants, so the objectives of the exercise must be worked out in advance. It should not be treated as a 'one size fits all' exercise. Many organizations spend time and effort looking for or even developing a reusable model. There is no Holy Grail; there may well be core themes that apply to all, but the process must be bespoke to the activity.

Kirkpatrick suggests that we:

- determine what we want to find out;
- use a written comment sheet with the items determined in the task above;
- design the sheet so that reactions can be tabulated and quantified;
- obtain honest reactions by making the sheet anonymous;
- allow participants to write additional comments not covered by the questions designed to be tabulated and quantified.

Two points emerge in relation to anonymity. First, anonymity does not necessarily promote honesty; it may merely allow other irrelevant agendas to come into play. Second, there is the view that knowing who wrote what allows a clear and targeted response. This underlines the point about each evaluation being bespoke to the activity. Kirkpatrick was writing long before optical mark reading (OMR) was widely available, but the technology makes the number-crunching significantly easier and faster.

There are many instances of training and developmental programmes being abandoned, running into the sand or being subject to inappropriate criticism because they were not seen as important or relevant by top managers. If this is the case, what were the programmes doing there anyway? Training and development actions should emerge as a result of the identification of organizational, departmental and individual needs. If that is evidently how they actually did emerge, the importance and relevance has been established so the critical managers are not conforming to agreed corporate policy and practice. (Although they will have agreed at all the appropriate meetings etc, giving rise to what the authors call 'public consensus and private disruption'.)

Kirkpatrick asserts that people must *like* a training programme to 'obtain the most benefit'. He quotes a former president of ASTD: 'It's not enough to say, "Here's the information, take it." We must make it interesting and motivate people to want to take it.'

Trainers, developers and managers should make their own appraisal of the training in order to supplement participants' reactions. The combination of two such evaluations is more meaningful than either one by itself. An example of this happening occurs in DHL, the express distributor company, when trainers and coaches get together periodically in groups to review a number of events and the reaction sheets before deciding if changes are necessary. Again, Kirkpatrick notes that although the results of this exercise may show whether the activity 'went well', there is no evidence that learning has taken place, that participants' working practice will be improved and that this improvement can be attributed to the training activity.

Step 2: Learning

The analysis of reactions enables the trainer/developer and the line manager to determine how well a programme or event was received. In addition, comments and suggestions will be obtained that will be helpful in enhancing the quality of future training and development actions and the various other services that support the process, such as catering and administration.

Although it's important to get a favourable response, favourable reactions 'don't assure learning'. Decisions on level, type and nature of future training and development actions and the resourcing of these actions are often based on the reactions of one or more key people.

We evidently do tend to pay more attention if the presenter is witty, stylish, well-prepared and uses state-of-the-art technology. However, if content is analysed it may possibly show that nothing of any real value was actually said! Therefore, argues Kirkpatrick, it's important to determine objectively the amount of learning that actually takes place. (Kirkpatrick uses a somewhat limited definition of learning here, ie what principles, facts, and techniques were understood and absorbed by trainees.) He offers the 'guideposts' shown in Table 9.2 for measuring learning.

Table 9.2 *Kirkpatrick's guideposts for measuring learning*

Measure the learning of each trainee so that quantitative results can be determined.

Use a before-and-after approach so that learning can be related to the programme.

As much as possible, the learning should be measured on an objective basis.

Where possible, use a control group (not receiving the training) to compare with the experimental group that receives the training.

Where possible, analyse the evaluation results statistically so that learning can be proven in terms of correlation or level of confidence.

Source: Kirkpatrick, 1959

Clearly, the evaluation of learning is more difficult than the evaluation of reaction. Like many later writers, Kirkpatrick argues that a knowledge of statistics is necessary for effective evaluation, although he does not necessarily believe that this evaluation should be done by development and training staff or equivalent. 'In many cases, the training department will have to call on a statistician to plan the evaluation procedures, analyse the data, and interpret the results.' Organizations operating under a transfer pricing system (see Chapter 10, Other Evaluation Tools, Techniques and Instruments) often have the evaluation function as completely separate, in terms of staffing, from the training and development function.

Kirkpatrick notes that 'it's relatively easy to measure learning that takes place in training on skills'. Evaluation of learning is incorporated into the process by setting up 'before-and-after situations in which trainees demonstrate whether they know the principles or techniques being taught'. In other words, clear criteria are set with regard to the expected outcomes. In *Managing for Investors in People* the authors produced a simple logbook format as a basis for agreeing objectives and evaluating learning and the application of that learning. It is reproduced here as Appendix 2.

Kirkpatrick recommends the use of testing when principles and facts rather than techniques are taught. He also counsels against the use of pre-prepared standardized tests and for the use of 'bespoke' material on the grounds that the external package will only be able to contribute to part of the overall evaluation. As an argument for securing departmental and organizational support, proving the effectiveness of training and development actions in terms of learning as well as reaction, evaluation of learning is demonstrably more powerful.

Step 3: Behaviour

Kirkpatrick tells this story:

> When I joined the Management Institute of the University of Wisconsin in 1949, one of my first assignments was to observe a one-week course on human relations for foremen and supervisors. I was particularly impressed by Herman, a foreman from a Milwaukee company. Whenever the instructor asked a question about human relations, Herman raised his hand. He had all the answers. I thought, 'If I were in industry, I'd like to work for someone like Herman.' It so happened that my cousin, Jim, worked at Herman's company and Herman was his boss. Jim told me that Herman may know all about the principles of human relations but he didn't practise them on the job. He performed as a typical 'bull-of-the-woods' who had little consideration for subordinates' feelings and ideas. I realized that there was a big difference between knowing principles and techniques and using them on the job.

Our experience suggests that, as with Herman above, *knowing* does not necessarily correlate with *doing*. The 'gap' is often between the real and stated rationale as to why the training is taking place; the ever-present struggle between rhetoric and reality. Those with responsibility for people management need to be very much aware of the culture of their organization and to be able to act on this knowledge.

Kirkpatrick offers the following criteria of desirable characteristics of individuals engaging on a development activity:

- *They must want to improve.*
- *They must recognize their own weaknesses.* This is a difficult one. We don't like the use of the word 'weakness' in this context; the focus should be on, and in the spirit of, continuous improvement.
- *They must work in a permissive climate.*
- *They must have help from someone who is interested and skilled.*
- *They must have an opportunity to try out new ideas.*

Evaluation of the result of training and development actions in terms of behaviour back at work is more difficult than reaction and learning evaluations. It requires a more scientific approach and the consideration of a range of factors. Again, Kirkpatrick offers 'guideposts', this time for evaluating training in terms of behavioural changes, as shown in Table 9.3.

Table 9.3 *Kirkpatrick's guideposts for evaluating training*

Appraise performance before and after the development action has taken place.

Have the appraisal conducted by peers, trainers, managers, supervisors, or any other colleague familiar with the individual's development. (The more the better.)

Statistically analyse the results to compare before-and-after performance and to relate such changes to the training and development actions.

Have a post-training appraisal three months or more after the training action so that participants have an opportunity to put into practice what they learnt. Subsequent appraisals may add to the validity of the study.

Use a control group.

Source: Kirkpatrick, 1959

Employee attitude surveys before and after training and development actions may be of use here (see Chapter 11, Attitude, Behaviour and Effectiveness). Material produced in support of actually achieving Investors in People status can, of course, be used; there are managers and employees surveys that can, and have been, easily adapted to all types and sizes of organizations.

To evaluate the impact of their own professional development activities it is necessary for managers and other staff to receive and give reflections of both peers and subordinates with regard to observed changes in practice. Upward appraisal and 360-degree appraisal can help here.

Step 4: Results

This is the most difficult area to evaluate effectively and Kirkpatrick recognized this. Although the objectives of most training and development actions can be stated in terms of outcomes, 'complicating factors can make it difficult, if not impossible, to evaluate certain kinds of programmes in terms of results' (Kirkpatrick, 1959).

Instructional training such as some elements of IT programmes lend themselves quite easily to a 'before-and-after' approach. It is easy to suggest that this is also true for more complex forms of development such professional skills development. For example, if an organizational priority was to increase positive customer response there are several ways in which this could be addressed. A training and development programme targeting sales teams could be arranged, as could a mentoring scheme utilizing the skills of senior staff with an excellent track record in selling. The before-and-after evaluation would simply count the number of sales. This falls into the trap of monocausality and could become a hostage to fortune. An improved level of sales could relate to external changes, internal changes, a new breakthrough in the area and so on.

In other words, there are so many variables it is difficult to tease them apart. It would be far easier – and more meaningful – to evaluate results in terms of the contribution made by training and development actions by using peer and self-assessment. Kirkpatrick advocated a participative approach to this level, noting that where it was applied it resulted in 'better feelings, attitudes, and other human relations factors'. He also predicted that there would be growing interest in this level in the future, although his hope was to be able to 'measure human relations training in terms of dollars'! It would be more appropriate to measure results in terms of an organization's capacity to learn, change and develop in line with its agreed objectives.

The effectiveness of line managers (and the training and development function) and those training and development activities that fall within their remit is obviously the key measure. However, to determine effectiveness, outcomes of training and development actions must be measured. The skills for this do not necessarily reside within training and development units, so consideration needs to be given to the developing of the developers or bringing in outside expertise, as many proponents of transfer pricing would argue.

CHAPTER 10

Other Evaluation Tools, Techniques and Instruments

This chapter offers a summary account of some of the main financial evaluation techniques. In addition it focuses on transfer pricing, a system that has been the subject of some attention and scrutiny in a number of organizations recently. Finally it looks briefly at various other instruments of evaluation.

Financial instruments

1. Cost-benefit analysis
The most often used of the financial measures. It is simply a comparison of all the costs of a training and development action against all the benefits. (It is important to note that many of these 'benefits' are estimated, so the securing of stakeholder agreement in advance is essential.) The calculation is:

NET BENEFIT = TOTAL BENEFIT – TOTAL COSTS

2. Return on investment (ROI)/Return on capital expended (ROCE)

The terms originate from accounting and usually refer to the pre-tax contribution measured against controllable assets. In terms of evaluation, ROI moves cost-benefit analysis up a gear.

$$ROI = [(BENEFITS - COSTS) \div COSTS] \times 100$$

3. Payback

Put simply, this looks at how long it will be before the total benefits of training and development actions exceed the total costs.

$$PAYBACK\ PERIOD = TOTAL\ INVESTMENT \div ANNUAL\ SAVINGS$$

4. Profitability

Profitability is basically net income; in other words, what is left over after every possible item of expenditure has been taken into account. In many organizations the single biggest spend is on staff costs. Evaluating productivity using this single largest factor in expenditure can be done in a number of ways including:

$$Profits\ per\ employee = \frac{Trading\ profits}{Number\ of\ employees}$$

$$Output\ per\ employee = \frac{Units\ produced\ or\ processed}{Number\ of\ employees}$$

$$\frac{Value\ added}{per\ employee} = \frac{Value\ added\ (sales\ revenue - cost\ of\ sales)}{Number\ of\ employees}$$

There are many definitions of value added; another could be the fraction of the market value added to the product by the organization's process. Generally it is the difference between turnover and the cost of bought-in materials.

Naturally, to claim that certain training and development actions are solely responsible for particular financial improvements is inappropriate and probably wrong. However, it is essential to be able to indicate contributions made.

5. Utility analysis

Utility is a function of the duration of a programme's effect on employees, the number of people trained, the validity of the training programme, the value of the activity for which the training was provided and the total cost of the programme (Phillips, 1991).

The formula for calculating this is:

$$\Delta U = T \ N \ dt \ Sdy - N \ C$$

and is probably deserving of an explanation . . .

Key

- ΔU = £ value of the development activity;
- T = duration and number of years of a development activity's impact on performance;
- N = Number of employees trained/developed;
- dt = True difference in job performance between the average trained/developed employees and the average untrained/undeveloped employees in units of standard deviation;
- Sdy = Standard deviation of performance of the untrained/undeveloped group in £;
- C = Cost of training/development per employee.

It is hard to see how this and similar formulae could be of any real value to most organizations. There are too many variables and defining such variables as the 'dt' element is unrealistic in the extreme except in a very limited number of cases.

6. Transfer pricing

Techniques such as transfer pricing are used to define and monitor the investment in staff development and training. It is appropriate here to examine this in some detail as a potentially useful strategy demonstrating to all the real cost and value of staff training and development, and to ensure that anecdotes and assumptions do not excessively inform management thinking. For example, there are many instances where senior staff assume that the employment of a trainer/staff developer means that that is exactly how they spend all their time – standing up in front of a group!

As the pressure on organizations to seek ways of doing more for less continues to increase, so the need to tie training and development more closely to organizational objectives becomes ever more important. Development and training departments are seen by many staff in organizations as a monopoly supplier and an overhead. It is clear, therefore, that there may be benefits from a system which increases the local sense of ownership (and therefore participation) and at the same time addresses organizational issues and clearly demonstrates value for money. Transfer pricing is worth examining in this context.

What is transfer pricing?

Transfer pricing is the pricing of services delivered by the training and development function and the charging of departments for the services they have received. In effect, therefore, the central spend is on training and development that is either a legal requirement (eg health and safety) or an organizational requirement (eg corporate and local induction, appraisal, etc). Other programmes are agreed with the appropriate unit and costs are clearly identified at the outset.

How is it implemented?

The first stage is initial costing. It is necessary to put a cost to *everything* relating to the delivery of training – including such activities as networking, advice, guidance and ad hoc discussions with colleagues that form the currently unquantifiable but essential soft benefit areas of development and training.

For the *totality* of a training or development action, what is the cost of:

- staff;
- accommodation;

- overheads;
- materials;
- equipment;
- external consultants/trainers?

The cost is calculated via the establishing of systems within the training and development function to track time spent. The result should be that departments understand the costs and, in understanding the costs, the need to justify provision by the soft benefits argument decreases dramatically. It is demonstrably clear that training and development is not a free commodity. There is the opportunity to give background information on the cost of services.

Start-up
Once key costs are calculated the consultation process can begin. This should aim to:

- agree with departments what will be provided;
- clarify the costs of the activities;
- identify any options on flexibility (for instance, if a department wanted a stress management programme it could be over one afternoon or take the form of an away-day);
- establish any spend limits;
- establish reporting back systems.

Operating in a transfer pricing environment
The process would be robust (supported by systems) and analytical. It should be able to cope with competition from outside the institution. Detailed monitoring is possible, with data broken down into, for example, courses, materials, consultancy, etc monitored departmentally, individually and institutionally.

What are the benefits?

- cost-consciousness;
- data on the real cost of services;
- talking directly to departments and teams;

- offering of costed options (reflecting the differential, spending power and priorities of individual units);
- feedback;
- enables clearer prioritization of services by staff development and clearer prioritization of training and development needs by line managers and their departments.

What are the long-term implications?

These include an increased likelihood of change in the size of the training and development function. Working relationships between the 'centre' and the line managers of departments should be enhanced. There would be separate funding of organizational initiatives and a concentration on short-term objectives. It would also be easier to identify inefficient providers of training and development and take appropriate action accordingly.

If training and development activities were costed in advance as described above, organizations would meet the twin objectives of increasing ownership at the local level and demonstrating cost effectiveness. Presumably all development would therefore be in line with corporate and business unit planning, very much in line with the requirements relating to maintaining and retaining Investors in People status.

Some other instruments

1. Pay forward

Pay forward is largely a response to the purely financial return instruments described above. It describes the benefits from training and development actions in terms of the organization's capacity to learn and change. Arguably this is a more appropriate model for 'not for profit' organizations. The benefits from pay forward cannot be expressed in financial terms. Benefits are in the form of cultural/behavioural change, increased staff identification with organizational objectives, observed changes in individual or team behaviour or other changes. The key is that investment in training is not made to produce an end in itself, but rather to improve the organization's ability to learn and change. Hence the notion that the benefits are 'projected into the future and cannot be identified separately from the outcomes of the wider change process'. The ultimate goal is to enable purely financial systems to 'fade into insignificance, since the training process is no longer separate from the business of managing' (Lee, 1996).

2. Impact analysis

In essence, impact analysis focuses on the importance of involvement of all key stakeholders prior to the delivery of the actual training and development. Having secured the involvement of all stakeholders, possibly in the form of a meeting or a working lunch, key objectives for the activity should be discussed and agreed, along with some agreement as to the areas for impact for follow-up evaluation. Clearly there are advantages in so far as stakeholder commitment and ownership can be built up and possible disadvantages in terms of the time needed from these stakeholders. The meeting should include all three of Stake's stakeholders: the agents, beneficiaries and victims (Stake, 1975). It is possible that some people will fall into more than one category. For example, a proposal regarding the development of a cross-organization team of staff with responsibility for training and development locally may make the training manager an agent (they will be facilitating the exercise), a victim (extra work/extra time/extra draw on resources) and a beneficiary (ultimately the improvement of training and development across the organization).

The standard method is to use Post-it notes or similar for people to write the two or three most important outcomes as they see it. The Post-its are collected, displayed on a wall and divided into related groups or themes. The themes are discussed and stakeholders are then given points to allocate to the theme or themes they believe represents the most important learning objectives.

When this exercise was undertaken by a major international oil company, the stakeholder group began by trying to agree what the key aspect, the 'defining act', of their business actually was, what it was that encapsulated and represented the sum of all their collected labours. To the surprise of many, it turned out to be the specific act of getting the petrol into the car!

The stakeholder group then discusses and makes suggestions for the evaluation strategy for each learning objective and the concomitant impact on organizational development and/or performance.

3. Trend

This is a simple statistical tool that can be used to look at possible relationships between data. When used in the evaluation of training and development this process looks at current trends in organizational (or unit) performance, forecasts performance and assesses the impact of learning on those trends. In essence, data relating to training and development actions would cover a number of analysis periods, say one year, and be converted from tables into a graph. The line through the data is the trend line.

4. The KPTM 10-stage model

This model, developed by Kearns and Miller, is linear – in contrast to the recent trend towards a cyclical approach. The model offers an excellent opportunity to define and focus the corporate evaluation process from a 'value added' perspective.

We have always said that the evaluation of *everything* is a waste of time. The KPTM model underlines this by arguing that there is a set of minimum skills that an employee can be expected to have. These are placed in Box 1. Those training and development activities that give 'added value' and/or 'market edge' are placed in Box 2. Only the contents of Box 2 are evaluated. The entire process comprises analysis, design, delivery and evaluation and is summarized as shown in Table 10.1.

Table 10.1 *The 10-stage model*

Stage	
1	Business needs
2	Analysis
3a	Design
3b	Design
4	Agree (back to 3b to amend as appropriate)
5	Delivery
6	Reaction
7	Learning
8	Transfer
9	Value added
10	Feedback

Table 10.2 *Evaluation methods*

	Scientific paradigm	'Alternative' paradigm	Synthesis – a paradigm of choices
Purpose	Summative	Formative	Intended use for intended users
Measurement	Quantative data	Qualitative data	Appropriate, credible, useful data
Design	Experimental design	Naturalistic enquiry	Creative, practical, situationally responsive designs
Researcher stance	Objectivity	Subjectivity	Fairness and balance
Enquiry mode	Deduction	Induction	Either or both
Conceptualization	Independent and dependent variables	Holistic interdependent system	Stakeholder questions and issues
Relationships	Distance, detachment	Closeness, involvement	Collaborative, consultative
Approach to study of change	Pre-post measures, time series, static portrayals at discrete points in time	Process-oriented, evolving capturing ongoing dynamism	Developmental, action-oriented, What needs to be known to get from where you are to where you want to be?
Relationship to prior knowledge	Confirmatory, hypothesis-testing	Exploratory, hypothesis-generating	Either or both

Sampling	Random, probabilistic	Purposeful, key informants	Combinations, depending on what information is needed
Primary approach to variations	Quantitative differences on uniform, standardized variables	Qualitative differences, uniqueness	Flexible: focus on comparisons most relevant to intended users and evaluation questions
Analysis	Descriptive and inferential statistics	Case studies, content and pattern analysis	Answers to stakeholders' questions
Types of statements	Generalizations	Context-bound	Extrapolations
Contribution to theory	Validating theoretical propositions from scientific literature	Grounded theory	Describing, exploring and testing stakeholders' and programme's theory of action
Goals	Truth, scientific acceptance	Understanding, perspective	Utility, relevance. Acceptance by intended users

Source: Adapted from Patton, 1997

What method?

The list of methods, instruments and strategies could be continued if not ad infinitum then for several more books! This would be pointless. The many hundreds of models and techniques will in the main merely repeat – using different terminology – much of what has gone before. We propose, therefore, to close this chapter by summarizing evaluation methods and to that end offer a table, slightly modified, originally prepared by Patton (1997). The 'scientific' method was originally dominant and most evaluation – if it took place at all – was of instructional-type training using the Kirkpatrick four levels or similar. The faith many managers place in apparently complex formulae is further evidence of this former dominance. A major theme of this book is neatly encapsulated in the phrase 'intended use for intended users' (see Table 10.2, goals, under synthesis).

CHAPTER 11

Attitude, Behaviour and Effectiveness

Once recognition has been achieved, many organizations find that this is the start, not the end of their continuous improvement journey. This chapter looks at how attitude, behaviour and effectiveness are linked and how strategies can be introduced in support of maintaining and retaining Investors in People. It is important at the outset to underline the difference between attitude and behaviour. An attitude is a predisposition to behave in a particular way, and behaviour relates to the individual's view as to what comprises the correct action for that particular situation at that particular time. Effectiveness would relate to success in achieving the objective of a higher rating by using the same resources better.

Was it good for you?

With regard to training and development, the method invariably used is to measure immediate reaction by multiple-choice questionnaires – the 'happy sheet'. Do we assume that because someone liked something they have learned something? In many cases it seems that we do. The happy sheet is the most commonly used form of evaluation in all types of organizations.

Indeed, there is little or no research evidence to support the notion that enjoying any form of training and development action means that learning has taken place and, more importantly, that it translates into better working practices. Additionally, an important function of the reaction sheet – providing feedback to services that support the training and development effort – is also often overlooked.

Is it important to find out whether people enjoyed themselves? It may well be, but there should be a clear rationale set out in advance as to why this is necessary and what the information gained is going to be used for. For example, there may be a wish to find out what type of programme appeals to what category of employee. Do office staff *like* different styles of training and development from technical staff? What variations exist between the learning styles of engineers and managers? Are there lessons to be learned in catering for different groups? There has been a great deal of research carried out into learning styles and their impact on learning, of which the most commonly used is that by Kolb and by Honey and Mumford.

Such information may well be gleaned by looking at people's attitude to the programme or event. The danger, of course, is that we treat these responses as though nothing else is impacting on the group.

David Lodge in his novel *Therapy* offers an interesting illustration of this. The main character, a scriptwriter, was very concerned that the studio audience response to his sitcom had been very poor. Only later did he learn that the audience had largely been made up of people from a factory that was to close, and they had all just received their redundancy notices with their pay packets.

Such evaluation techniques may be used to work out when the best times to hold a particular event are. Normally this will show you that about 50 per cent of people feel themselves to be too busy to spare any time during the week and opt for weekend conferences and a different 50 per cent become apoplectic at the thought of having to go to a conference at a weekend. It will be the same with trying to build in leisure time for the longer residential programme. Roughly half the people will demand it if it isn't there and the other half will tell you they are not there for a holiday, if there is free time.

Evaluating the one-/two-day event at the end of the session is often a waste of time. People are anxious to go (some will have gone), some may be reluctant to offend, others will think it their duty to offend, some may not wish to speak at all. Besides, the end is too late to make adjustments anyway. In essence, it is the personalities of the participants that come through in the main, rather than how good or bad or useful the actual event has been.

Attitudes

These instruments and techniques should be approached with extreme caution. They can go badly wrong, especially where the participants are well qualified and articulate. It is essential to ensure that presenters are in possession of both knowledge and skills at an appropriately higher level.

1. The attitude training process

The evaluation process divides up into five complementary parts as described below. As a convenient vehicle, we use as an example a group of university teachers who are being introduced to teaching observation.

a. What is wanted?

Here, there must be agreement as to what attitudes are sought and how they will lead to some form of individual, group or organizational improvement. Such attitudes will by definition be general. Resolving to feel less hostile to the notion of other people being in the lecture theatre other than the students is one example.

b. Where are we now?

The group is invited to self-assess their current working practices. These are then set against the 'ideal'. The group may have concerns about confidentiality. Some may view the development as a management ploy to root out the 'weaker' members; others may be enthusiastic but apprehensive; and still others may resent the intrusion of the event and its expected outcomes on their research activities.

c. Why do we want to get there?

This is basically a selling job. Participants, rightly, have to be convinced that the desired attitudes are 'right'. Observation and feedback is useful professionally, is popular with assessors and auditors of all types and the ultimate beneficiary is the student.

d. How do we get there?

Techniques and strategies via role play/group work/video packages/ guest speakers/student views on teaching and learning.

e. How do we know we've got there?

The behaviour at work reflects the 'new' attitude. People recognize the individual and team benefits; the practice of observation takes root as part of the 'life' of the department. New staff are locally inducted into the system. The activity is not seen as a bolt-on, management-led activity.

2. The repertory grid

Basically this involves finding out what people think about a particular skill or attribute and what comprises 'good practice'. The technique was developed by a psychologist, George Kelly, and was designed to elicit a respondent's view of a particular issue, item or situation. Respondents produce their own list of constructs (characteristics) on which they rate items – such as colleagues. The resulting construct and item grid can then be used to describe how the respondent sees the particular issue, item or situation. The repertory grid is normally done on a one-to-one basis but works very well in groups – and given that most sessions would not be able to support the amount of time for one-to-one sessions it is the group form that is suggested here.

The example group for this technique is senior managers brought together for a session on equal opportunities. To begin with, it is necessary to find out what they mean by equal opportunities, so they are asked to think of colleagues who display (in their view) positive attributes, negative attributes and indifferent attributes in this area and to write down what these are. The facilitator does not define or discuss equal opportunities at this stage. The names of these colleagues are written down on cards and given a number from 1 to 6. The cards are shuffled and the participants are invited to draw out cards 1 to 3. The facilitator asks them to consider reactions these three may have to given situations where equal opportunities is an issue. Who would do what and why would they do it? What are the differences/similarities? (The focus throughout the whole process is on what these colleagues *do*, not on what they *are*.) There then follows a closely supervised process of selecting people who are expected to show quite different reactions followed by participants representing this on a prepared continuum showing, for example, attitudes ranging from open to hostile, supportive to unsupportive, tolerant to intolerant and so on. Participants will continue and compare and contrast different combinations of senior managers. When each manager in this example has been included in six comparisons, it should be clear how each participant sees equal opportunities. A score can then be given to their comparisons and so the repertory grid is constructed and used to reflect back at the individual and the group not only what the individual thinks about the issues but what they as a group feel is best or most appropriate practice. The repertory grid process can be both complex and complicated. For evaluation purposes it is best kept as simple as possible.

Behaviour scales

These are used to establish what changes are expected from training and development actions and offer criteria by which these changes, if any, can be measured. Appraisal/performance review offers an excellent opportunity to introduce behaviour scales.

A simple example would be an agreed improvement in quantity and quality of output. Development measures set in motion at the appraisal/review might include some classroom-based activities, assigning a mentor from within the department with extensive experience in the area, reviewing time-management skills in order to agree and establish time targets. The individual would then keep a record of how they felt they were improving, along the lines of a reflective journal or learning log that could form part of the individual's preparation for appraisal. This method clearly offers the opportunity to make pre- and post-development action comparisons that have real and evident meaning for all parties. The organization has, therefore, a clear 'audit trail' (well suited to the new reassessment model) demonstrating the value of a development action. A hypothetical example of the use of behaviour scales follows.

A group of managers in an engineering company were seen to be in need of developmental support to improve their interpersonal skills. Their technical background was, in the main, exemplary, but they had been flung into the management arena, given a set of tasks, responsibilities and expectations and left to sink. Behavioural scales were selected as the most appropriate tool as the organization wished to have some indication as to the perceived success of the training and development activity and also, given the highly political nature of the action and the cause of the action, to give it a high profile by involvement of a large number of people at all levels. See Table 11.1, The Key Stages.

The intended outcome was that there would be evidence of enhanced efficiency and this was achieved. An unintended outcome was that there was a more coherent and cohesive working relationship between not only the line managers themselves but also with the human resources department (HR).

Measuring changes in effectiveness

Measuring the impact that training and development actions have made should take place at three levels: organizational, departmental/team and individual. There is sometimes a tendency by management, even after recognition, to see the bottom-line figure as the only real indicator of success or failure. Looking at a far broader set of critical success factors has long been advocated. Blake and Mouton (1964) looked for high *production*-centred management practices coterminous with high *people*-centred management practices. Critical success factors can be used in any environment. Bramley (1996) cites Cameron (1980) as providing a very useful classification of organizational effectiveness when discussing training and development evaluation with management.

Table 11.1 *The key stages*

1.   Staff opinions were sought via a survey. The questionnaire explored perceptions of managers' commitment to their staff and competence on delivering the requirements of their role. Questions on communication, consideration, management skills, teamworking, creating development opportunities, coaching, supporting and consulting were grouped together under various appropriate headings (at least 10 in each category to enhance reliability) and respondents rated them on a five-point scale from never to always.

2.   The line managers were given a summary of the responses, expressed anonymously, as answers to the questions asked in the survey. They were rated on a five-point scale from 'agree' to 'disagree'. The feedback was discussed at board level and after at a meeting of the managers with members of the human resources department (HR), who had been responsible for conducting the survey and arranging the feedback.

3.   A development programme was agreed. Part of this was to be classroom-based where there was a critical mass of low scores – as in financial management and people-management skills, and part was via a raft of other strategies – mentoring, short secondments, exchanges inside and outside the company, team building activities.

4.   One year on – and following the end of the final, 'wash-up' session, a second survey was conducted and improvements – or otherwise – were therefore measurable. Chi-squared percentages were used to compare the year on year changes.

Table 11.2 *Bramley's matrix*

	Individual (my work)	Work group (my section)	Function (my department)	Regional level	Organizational level
Goal-directed					
Resource-acquiring					
Satisfying constituencies					
Internal processes					

The four categories of organizational effectiveness

1. Goal-directed

Here the focus is on output and achievement or otherwise of objectives, eg improvements in output, training staff in the use of new software, improving communications.

2. Resource-acquiring

Here effectiveness is assessed by the level to which the organization 'acquires needed resources from its external environment' (Bramley, 1996), eg external contracts.

3. Constituencies

As the word implies, these are basically customer or client groups who are in some way stakeholders. Effectiveness is evaluated in terms of 'how well the organization responds to the demands and expectations of these groups', eg audit and inspection.

4. Internal process

The focus here is on aspects of organizational structure and culture such as stress levels, trust, information flow. Bramley (1996) uses these categories as the basis from which to build a matrix, which is reproduced as Table 11.2.

These evaluation instruments are of great potential value if used with care and expertise and can be applied with equal success to any category of employee. Constraints include time and resources. It is worth reiterating that the skills and knowledge needed to conduct the development, delivery and analysis do not always reside in training and development and/or personnel departments in many organizations.

CHAPTER 12

How Well Are We Doing?

In this chapter we build on the previous three chapters and offer the reader a variety of strategies aimed at teasing out the business benefits of training and development actions. Table 12.1 gives a slightly modified version of Kirkpatrick's four-level evaluation model, adapted to include measuring for return on investment.

The context, input, reaction and outcome (CIRO) approach

A broad approach to classifying evaluation was taken by Warr, Bird and Rackham (1970). The four areas of Context, Input, Reaction and Outcome evaluation can be summarized as follows:

- *Context evaluation* involves deciding whether there is a need for any action, basing that decision on management information. Objectives are agreed in three categories: the ultimate objective and two intermediate objectives relating to changes in behaviour and acquisition of new skills.
- *Input evaluation* basically decides on the best method of delivery, taking into account such factors as mode, timing and style of delivery, level and type involvement of staff, financial factors.

Table 12.1 *Kirkpatrick's four-level model, adapted*

Level	Questions
Reaction and planned action	What are participants' reactions to the training? What do they plan to do with the material?
Learning	What skills, knowledge or attitudes have changed? By how much?
On-the-job application	Did participants apply on the job what they learned in training?
Business results	Did the on-the-job applications produce measurable results?
Return on investment	Did the monetary value of the results exceed the cost of training and/or development action?

- *Reaction evaluation* is, as its name suggests, used to determine participants' reactions based on individual reports or interviews.
- *Outcome evaluation* uses the results to inform future planning, notably with regard to the formulation of general and specific objectives and the setting of criteria by which success will be measured.

Critics of Kirkpatrick assert that the four-level training evaluation process may not always produce genuinely meaningful, long-term results. Consequently planning with regard to evaluation may operate within inappropriately limited parameters. The result is a reduction in the organization's ability to conduct relevant and useful evaluations.

Kirkpatrick's model implies that conducting an evaluation is a standardized, pre-packaged process. This clearly is not always the case, nor is it desirable to present evaluation as something which produces facts, as opposed to management information on achievement or otherwise of organizational targets.

Some myths

There is a range of issues raised by those comments. Several of these issues can be categorized as myths. Table 12.2 gives some myths about evaluation.

Trainers and those with people-development responsibility should not employ the model without assessing needs and resources. Actual application of the results can also be a neglected area. Critics suggest that when the Kirkpatrick model is used as a universal framework for all evaluations, it can be the *model itself* that is shaping the process and, therefore, the results.

Table 12.2 *Some myths about evaluation*

Myth	Comment
An evaluation is definitive	Most evaluation activity appears to believe in monocausality. In other words a single evaluation action can be used to answer all questions (one size fits all). We do not appear to be prepared for ambiguous findings. Nor is much attention paid to the impact of varying levels of methodological rigour. Credibility and accuracy are not established and maintained by one type of evaluation.
To evaluate is to be effective	Questions must be asked and an agenda agreed before any action is taken. Why is the evaluation taking place? Who wants it? Why do they want it? What are they planning to do with the information?
Trainers and developers are responsible and/or accountable for effectiveness	Greater attention should be given clarifying exactly what the training department is responsible for and therefore accountable for. Clear criteria should be agreed at the outset

Table 12.2 *(continued)*

Myth	Comment
	as to what comprises effectiveness. Being held accountable for quality of content, for example, may or may not be appropriate. The people best placed to support and assess the transfer of learning are those staff with people management responsibilities. The role of staff development is to support this process.
Kirkpatrick's level four, impact on the organization, is the most important	We do not see any level as having superiority over another. Although clear links, they measure different things. Measures employed for one level are not necessarily transferable to another.
Quantification is essential	No, it isn't. However, agreement on what the organization hopes to get out of the activity and how this will be measured is essential. In other words, success criteria can be both quantitative and qualitative, but these criteria are agreed by all stakeholders in advance.

Bernthal's Seven Steps

Bernthal (1995) identifies seven steps in the setting up of a 'long distance', in-depth evaluation programme. These are shown in Table 12.3.

Step 1. Identify the organization's values and practices

Most organizations have mission or vision statements. These statements are not always perceived as being put into practice. In

Table 12.3 *Bernthal's seven steps*

Step 1:   Identify the organization's values and practices.
Step 2:   Identify skills, knowledge, and attitudes.
Step 3:   Define the scope and purpose of the evaluation.
Step 4:   Identify data sources.
Step 5:   Choose the best method for collecting data.
Step 6:   Select the best measurement approach.
Step 7:   Gather and inventory your resources.

identifying organizations' actual core values it is necessary to link them to *actual* practices. If, for example, one of the stated values is 'teamwork', does it occur in reality? If so, are individual objectives linked to departmental objectives and those departmental objectives linked back to a declared organizational value of teamwork?

Step 2. Identify skills, knowledge, and attitudes

Having made the link between policy and practice, it is then easier to identify the type of activity that will enable staff to improve performance in such a climate. To facilitate this, production of a list of skills and knowledge requirements linked to the identified practices can be undertaken.

If analysis of training and development needs is not a regular feature of the organization, then the following will need to be taken into consideration. Training needs analysis (TNA) is sometimes seen as a logical starting point for the evaluation process, in tandem with strategic planning. The TNA should seek to identify the following:

- the knowledge and skills the training or development action needs to address;
- a profile of the target audience in terms of learning experiences and preferences, attitudes, range of existing knowledge and skills, personal attributes, previous work based experience and so on;

- non-training/development issues which may impact upon performance;
- training/development related issues that may impact on the mastery of objectives and on the transfer of learned skills/knowledge into practice.

Step 3. Define the scope and purpose of the evaluation

Having established how training and development 'fits' within an organization, a series of questions can be generated. Effective evaluation should, it is argued, measure more than the Kirkpatrick levels of reaction, learning, behaviour and results. Those levels focus primarily on outcomes and do not take into account *processes* leading to the results.

There are several areas beyond Kirkpatrick's four levels that can be evaluated. These include:

- the quality, delivery, and/or retention of the training and development action;
- whether the training and development action solved a problem or an issue for a particular group of staff;
- how useful 'parallel' training and development is for managers and their staff (eg appraisal – appraiser and appraisee);
- variables in the work environment that discourage or facilitate the effect of training and development actions;
- organizational context – there are barriers that hinder and factors that encourage and support the training and development effort.

A useful exercise is to list the barriers to training and development and those factors that encourage, support and enhance training and development and then to set these alongside the potential outcomes of pursuing this route. Focus groups or similar drawn from identified key stakeholders can be used in support of this process.

Step 4. Identify data sources

The quality of evaluation data depends on the source. Criteria for choosing the best sources of data include objectivity, accessibility, and reliability. Sources should be:

- unbiased;
- able to provide understandable information;
- easy to access; and
- able to produce uncontaminated information.

Step 5. Choose the best method for collecting data

Any *appropriate* research methodology can be employed. The emphasis on appropriateness relates to Juran's fitness for purpose and practical limitations.

Step 6. Select the best measurement approach

If the methods employed to evaluate a training and development action are simplistic, or if only one method is employed, the result will not be objective and subject to critical review, justified and/or unjustified, thus devaluing any impact it may have. Therefore, to increase objectivity, a variety of methods and approaches should be employed.

Step 7. Gather and inventory your resources

Finally, identify the people who will assist in the evaluative process. What are their skills? Which parts of the process should they be responsible for? Do they have enough power and influence in the organization to act on and implement salient outcomes?

The 'endless belt' of development

The UK Industrial Society (1994) recommends this method of evaluation. It incorporates validation and encourages a cyclical approach as follows:

- defining objectives that relate to business needs;
- designing an appropriate learning process;
- assessing the performance of participants before and after the learning process;
- measuring the lasting benefits for the individual and for the organization.

Table 12.4 *The endless belt of development*

Stage	Activity	Comments
Stage 1	Recognize a business need	This might be a particular target, eg dealing with a problem such as levels of complaints, or launching a new activity or a reorganization. A business need does not always generate a training and development action.
Stage 2	Define development objectives	This should be done via appropriate consultation and discussion with stakeholders, the key players being the line manager and the provider/ facilitator of the action.
Stage 3	Design learning process	An appropriate route is agreed – perhaps offsite and classroom-based, perhaps assigning a mentor, perhaps a short secondment, perhaps an NVQ. Wherever possible, ensure the method is 'bespoke' to the learner.
Stage 4	Experience learning process	Typically, the participant will be given several opportunities to reflect and absorb, possibly including the recording of views in a reflective journal or training logs. Reaction sheets and questionnaires will also be used. The reaction sheet will validate the event by checking that what was intended to be covered was covered and the question-naire will measure learning before application. (A test can also be used.)
Stage 5	Use and reinforce learning	In essence this is the key to embedding the new learning into working practices. The line manager is the key player here and will agree actions to ensure embedding.

Table 12.4 *(continued)*

Stage	Activity	Comments
Stage 6	Judge benefit to the organization	At least several months after the completion of the training and development action, the impact on the organization should be assessed. This should be done by comparing Stages 2 and 5, ie the link between development objectives and operationalization. Outcomes, including examples of return on investment if appropriate, are fed back in to Stage 1, and the 'endless belt' continues.

The 'endless belt' comprises six stages as shown in Table 12.4 above. Devotees claim that it does not clash with other approaches, such as Kirkpatrick's and that it is better because 'it starts earlier'.

The Institute of Personnel Development (IPD) has produced what might be seen as a developed version of the endless belt in the form of a tool kit. It divides into two sections. In the first section, an overview of the organizational benefits of investing in learning is set out. The second section 'works through a model of the process of investing in learning and evaluating the impact of that investment'.

The IPD uses Kirkpatrick's four levels, but includes material on establishing parameters, setting the learning objectives and measuring the return on investment. Level 4 is 'evaluating the impact on business performance' and includes guidance on the following methods:

- structured interviews with senior management;
- senior management estimate of benefits;
- trend line analysis;
- impact analysis;
- organizational elements model;
- control group and pilots;
- management information.

In essence, we have come full circle. Those criticisms levelled at Kirkpatrick described earlier in this chapter could also be made to apply here (especially the myths). That would not be constructive. If all organizations in the UK at least followed Kirkpatrick, billions of pounds would be saved every year.

CHAPTER 13

The Responsive Organization

The goal-based evaluation methods of Kirkpatrick have fallen out of favour somewhat over the past 20 years. This is largely due to the growth in awareness, interest and understanding with regard to the highly political nature of evaluation and the selection and use of evaluation strategies. A narrow definition of responsive evaluation would be limited to finding out the views of stakeholders and presenting them in a useable format. Our definition includes the whole range of types of evaluation set in the context of what the organization wants/needs combined with the best methods of meeting these wants/needs. Therefore, responsive evaluation can make use of any strategy, having first secured agreement on purpose and function (ie intended use by intended users).

Some examples of evaluation 'types' are shown in Table 13.1.

Stake (1975) coined the phrase *'responsive evaluation'* and argues that evaluation is concerned more with the interests of the various stakeholders. (His three types of stakeholder are, somewhat alarmingly, *agents, beneficiaries and victims!* Set this in context with the [mis]use of business process re-engineering recently to downsize/rightsize/de-layer/flatten structures.) The interests of the stakeholders are divided into *claims, concerns* and *issues*. The first

Table 13.1 *Some examples of evaluation 'types'*

Type	Description
Compliance	Legal, sectoral or organizational requirements
Criterion-focused	Quality, stakeholder satisfaction
Developmental	The manager/trainer (evaluator) is part of the group that designs/develops/delivers the training or development action
External	Independent specialists are used, often to enhance credibility
Goal-based	
Longitudinal	A study of participants and training and development actions over a period of time
Norm referenced	
Participatory	Direct involvement of participants, as in a review of peer observation of teaching by the group itself
Process	Day-to-day operational issues and improvement of services in support of the delivery of training and development actions
Quality assurance	

task for the evaluator, therefore, is to identify who the stakeholders actually are.

Legge (1984) writing on the evaluation of planned organizational change notes that in addition to most research in this area being badly designed, rigorous evaluation research is so limited in scope as to be of little value to anyone. Rather than attempt such obviously flawed practice, a contingent approach should be adopted, asking questions relating to purpose and methodology. Bramley (1996) summarizes these as four key questions and we have modified them to broaden their scope as follows:

- Do you want the proposed training and development action to be evaluated?
- What functions do you wish the evaluation to serve?
- Which approach (list alternatives) best suits the requirements of the activity?
- To what extent are constraints resulting from this approach acceptable?

What is meant by responsive evaluation?

Current evaluation strategies tend to emphasize quantitative data rather than qualitative data to demonstrate worth or value. The most popular measure is to monitor participant reaction to training and development actions, on a numerical scale, with the ubiquitous 'happy sheet' or reaction sheet.

With the exception of classroom-based instructional-type training activities, justifying effectiveness of training and development actions appears to be one or more of a set of measures that apply a numerical/financial 'value' on the results of the activity. Typical financial methods such as cost benefit analysis and return on investment and others are described in Chapter 10, Other Evaluation Tools, Techniques and Instruments.

If these are the only measures employed, evaluation may well run into the sand insofar as it is very unlikely that it can be satisfactorily proven that a particular training programme or development action has actually caused any benefits claimed. Often, proof is impossible to find; too many other variables are in play and, of course, nothing is monocausal. However, linking training and development actions to individual, departmental and organizational outcomes is absolutely essential. The process of creating such a link is ambiguous and highly interpretative, and becomes more complicated the more complex the organization. When evaluating training and development, the critical activity is the collection of evidence that suggests and preferably demonstrates a causal relationship between action and results. The creativity is in developing that link.

A responsive evaluation strategy can be made to pay attention to both 'hard' and 'soft' issues. It does not minimize the importance of showing outcome-oriented results of training but does recognize that perceptions about training and development are shaped by many qualitative factors. Phillips (1991) describes responsive evaluation as a 'both/and' approach, rather than an 'either/or' approach. It is both quantitative and qualitative; it is both summative and formative. It deals with process as well as outcome.

It is a really a question, again, of fitness for purpose. Sometimes quantitative, outcome-oriented information is more effective, and other times qualitative, process-oriented information is more effective. The key is paying attention to the political nature of the organization.

The model has as its objective the transferring of information to stakeholders so that they can act on the results. In order to be useful, any information must be translated so that it is meaningful to the people who are being informed. Everyone will perceive and respond to given information in a different way; therefore it is difficult to assess in advance exactly what, if anything, will be meaningful to them.

Stake argues that responsive evaluation recognizes the personal and political aspects of decision making. If responsive evaluation is to be employed effectively, there are certain basic 'rules' that we believe must be employed in order for it to be beneficial. These are:

- Know your organization – and be known in it.
- Be especially well informed with regard to those who allocate funding or contribute to the funding of staff development.
- Don't produce huge amounts of data.
- Incorporate the data into user-friendly material for stakeholders.
- In preparing material, keep in mind who will be using the information and for what purpose(s).

Who are the stakeholders?

They should be identified at the earliest opportunity. Who is involved and in what capacity from the outset? Who should be involved? Who thinks they ought to be involved and isn't (and so on)? Ask three key questions of the stakeholders, whether self-styled or actual, as shown in Table 13.2.

This element of the process should enable useful communication to take place between the manager/trainer and the stakeholders.

Table 13.2 *Stakeholder questions*

Why is this training and development action important to them?

What actually is their stake in it?

What values, biases or experiences might influence their judgement about the programme?

What are the stakeholders' information needs?

Basically:

- What do they want to know?
- Why do they want to know it? and
- What are they going to do with the information?

If the various stakeholders can be brought together as a group this will also offer the advantage of starting to create a degree of uniformity and, indeed, ownership of the activity. Phillips (1991) suggests we find out what questions the stakeholders themselves have. If they have no questions about a training and development action, they are unlikely to be interested in, or use, any evaluative information in whatever form it is presented.

Most organizations are going through a time of great change, so more than ever the manager/trainer needs to have direct access to at least one key decision maker. This direct access should enable greater awareness of political factors and the various inevitable 'hidden agendas'.

What data?

Collecting *and using* both quantitative and qualitative methods to evaluate training and development actions will improve the managers'/developers' ability to get actions implemented. Responsive evaluation can also measure quantitative elements of training and development actions.

Many senior managers prefer quantitative information because they believe that it represents hard, objective data. Of course this is not necessarily the case. There is also no reliable way to gather quantitative data on some important aspects of training or development. The end result is often a combination of guesswork and invention, and is therefore relatively meaningless. The point to be made is, make the number-crunching 'purposeful and thereby meaningful, as opposed to not doing it'. Therefore, when the advantages and disadvantages of quantitative and qualitative data are known, managers can encourage stakeholders to focus on the agreed important issues.

Clearly, for instance, quantified data will give no indication of attitude change or a rise or fall in morale. It is absolutely necessary, therefore, to look at *meaning*:

- What does the training and development action *mean* to participants?
- What does it *mean* to the core business of the organization?

Measurement of quality is often descriptive and comes in forms such as anecdotes, case studies or 'audit trails'. Different methodologies are employed in the gathering of different types of data. Phillips (1991) points out that numerical data that are tied to business results are often monitored through such methods as 'surveys, productivity measures (such as the sales volume, the size of an average sale, or the number of incentive bonuses), and quality measures (such as reductions in error, waste, rework, or customer complaints)'.

Qualitative data is gathered via such methods as interviews, focus groups, observations, or open-ended questionnaires. This allows for anecdotes, audit trails and so on to be collected in order broaden the evaluation of specific training and development actions, such as examples of how new skills and/or knowledge are being applied (Kirkpatrick Level 3, 1958, 1959).

Of course the obvious criticism of qualitative data is that it can be seen as subjective, but relying solely or too heavily on either type of data can easily result in inaccurate conclusions being drawn by stakeholders and the training and development function itself. Qualitative measures have made something of a comeback in the

UK over recent years, not least because of the impact of Investors in People itself where audit trails, essentially triangulated anecdotes, are used as an effective means of assessing organizations against the national Standard.

Quantitative measures are equally subject to charges of misuse. Such measures can be outcome-oriented without providing any insight into the area of inquiry. Regardless of declared interest in statistical data, anecdotal material often holds more sway.

Individual items of such information may not be seen to be of value. It is the synergy generated by linking the results so as to form constructive and useable information for stakeholders that is of real and demonstrable value. Meaning can be enhanced by paying close attention to how the various parameters are set. The same information can be made to look very different depending on how it is made to 'stand out'. For senior staff, the information should be framed in terms of strategic objectives, but managers might also want to highlight certain other real concerns.

The key message here is to know your audience and to package information accordingly. Stakeholders should continue to be involved and informed throughout the planning cycle. All feedback offered should feed into the decisions behind the strategic management of the organization, providing the necessary clear link between development and management.

Feedback is not limited to verbal or written forms. There is increasing interest in electronic forms. E-mail, for example, as an interactive evaluative tool can be used at a variety of levels and in a variety of ways, as can organizations' Web pages or local Intranet.

Decisions are the product of a variety of interrelated factors – opinion, fact, information, internal influence, external influence and so on – plus all of the personal 'baggage' brought to any decision making process. Therefore, the best way to contribute to and influence that decision is to share information with stakeholders continuously.

Why bother?

We used this question as a chapter title in *Investors in People Explained*. It is also applicable here as many organizations still don't evaluate effectively or even at all. A responsive evaluation

Table 13.3 *Categories of evaluation*

Easterby-Smith (1994)	
Proving	Demonstrating something has happened because of training actions
Improving	Something becomes better than it currently is
Learning	Evaluation is an integral part of the development process
Control	Relating training actions to organizational objectives
Bramley (1996)	
Feedback evaluation	Provides 'quality control over the design and delivery of training activities'
Control evaluation	Relates 'training policy and practice to organizational goals'
Research evaluation	Seeks to 'add to knowledge of training and practice in a way that will have more general application than feedback evaluation'
Intervention	
Power games	

strategy can help direct others' knowledge, perception and understanding of training and development. Focusing on the stakeholders, it links training and development to the wider goals and objectives of the organization. It is the job of the manager to provide enough evidence for that link to be established and for it to continue and strengthen. Therefore who the stakeholders are and what they want to know must be clarified at the outset, and only then should the appropriate evaluation instruments be selected.

It is again appropriate to reiterate that evaluation is not the last thing to be done – it must be the first. Criteria must be set prior to any training and development actions, and these actions must relate back to the departmental plan and thence to the organization's strategic plan.

What should be evaluated?

What *should* be evaluated depends on what the purpose of the evaluation is. This will also clearly impact on strategies and techniques used. Two useful examples of categories of evaluation are shown in Table 13.3.

In essence, therefore, responsive evaluation asks the key question: *Why should we evaluate?* We may wish to measure changes in attitudes, behaviour, skills knowledge or effectiveness. We may have a raft of other motives, some open, some less so. It is extremely likely that there will be several, often competing, reasons for undertaking the evaluation of anything and training and development is no exception. It is essential to 'know' your own organization in terms of how decisions actually get made. In other words, to be able to tease out the reality not the rhetoric.

Once you have worked out to what sort of organization you belong then an appropriate strategy can be worked out. The responsive model offers flexibility, depth and continuity, with managers and others with responsibility for training and development contributing to the agenda of the organization rather than being victims of it.

Any form of evaluation must have as its *raison d'être* the intention of being *used as intended by the intended users*. Anything else is a waste of resources.

The National Standard for Effective Investment in People

Principle One: Commitment

An Investor in People makes a commitment from the top to develop all employees to achieve its business objectives.

1.1 The commitment from top management to train and develop employees is communicated effectively throughout the organization.

1.2 Employees at all levels are aware of the broad aims or vision of the organization.

1.3 The employer has considered what employees at all levels will contribute to the success of the organization, and has communicated this effectively to them.

1.4 Where representative structures exist, communication takes place between management and representatives on the vision of where the organization is going and the contribution that employees (and their representatives) will make to its success.

Principle Two: Planning

An Investor in People regularly reviews the needs and plans the training and development of all employees.

2.1   A written but flexible plan sets out the organization's goals and targets.

2.2   A written plan identifies the organization's training and development needs, and specifies what action will be taken to meet these needs.

2.3   Training and development needs are regularly reviewed against goals and targets at the organization, team and individual level.

2.4   A written plan identifies the resources that will be used to meet training and development needs.

2.5   Responsibility for training and developing employees is clearly identified and understood throughout the organization, starting at the top.

2.6   Objectives are set for training and development actions at the organization, team and individual level.

2.7   Where appropriate, training and development needs are linked to external standards such as National Vocational Qualifications (NVQs) or Scottish Vocational Qualifications (SVQs) and units.

Principle Three: Action

An Investor in People takes action to train and develop individuals on recruitment and throughout their employment.

3.1   All new employees are introduced effectively to the organization and all employees new to a job are given the training and development they need to do that job.

3.2   Managers are effective in carrying out their responsibilities for training and developing employees.

3.3   Managers are actively involved in supporting employees to meet their training and development needs.

3.4   All employees are made aware of the training and development opportunities open to them.

3.5   All employees are encouraged to help identify and meet their job-related training and development needs.

3.6   Action takes place to meet the training and development needs of individuals, teams and the organization.

Principle Four: Evaluation

An Investor in People evaluates the investment in training and development to assess achievement and improve future effectiveness.

4.1   The organization evaluates the impact of training and development actions on knowledge, skills and attitude.

4.2   The organization evaluates the impact of training and development actions on performance.

4.3   The organization evaluates the contribution of training and development to the achievement of its goals and targets.

4.4   Top management understands the broad costs and benefits of training and developing employees.

4.5   Action takes place to implement improvements to training and development identified as a result of evaluation.

4.6   Top management's continuing commitment to training and developing employees is demonstrated to all employees.

Evaluation of Training and Development Effectiveness

Name ....

Section/Department ....

Part A: Prior to the training or development action

1. Proposed training/development activity.

2. Details, eg dates, locations, cost, etc.

3. The business objective the proposed activity will help to achieve.

4. What skills and/or knowledge will be learnt as a result of the activity?

5. How will the new skills and/or knowledge be applied after the activity?

6. Line manager's comments, ie expectations in terms of targets or standards.

Signatures .... Participant .... date

.... Line Manager .... date

Part B: Immediately after the training and/or developmental activity

1. Did the participant attend? Yes/no (if no give reason).

2. To what extent has this activity met the agreed training and/or developmental need?

Please circle   Not at all   1   2   3   4   Totally

Comments

3. How will the learning be applied?

4. What help/support is needed to put the learning into practice?

5. To what extent did the activity represent:

Value for money?

Please circle Not at all 1 2 3 4 Totally

An acceptable standard of delivery?

Please circle   Not at all   1   2   3   4   Totally

Comments

6. Agreed date to review ....

Signatures .... Participant .... date

.... Line Manager .... date

Part C: Review to monitor impact on performance

1. How has the learning been applied since the activity?

2. To what extent have the agreed objectives/targets or standards been met?

Please circle   Not at all   1   2   3   4   Totally

Comments

3. If learning has not been applied please state why.

4. What further action or review is required?

Signatures .... Participant .... date

.... Line Manager .... date

References

Bernthal, P (1995) Evaluation that goes the distance, *American Journal of Training and Development*, **49**, p 41

Blake, R R and Mouton, J S (1964) *The Managerial Grid*, Gulf, Houston

Bramley, P (1996) *Evaluating Training Effectiveness*, 2nd edn, McGraw-Hill, New York

Cameron, K (1980) Critical Questions in Assessing Organisational Effectiveness, *Organisational Dynamics*, pp 66–80, Autumn

Easterby-Smith, M (1994) *Evaluation of Management Education, Training and Development*, 2nd edn, Gower, Aldershot

Honey, P and Mumford, A (1992) *Manual of Learning Styles*, P Honey, Maidenhead

Juran, J M (1988) *Juran on Planning for Quality*, Free Press, New York

Kearns, P and Miller, T (1996) *Training Measurement and Evaluation*, Technical Communications Publishing Ltd, Hitchin

Kirkpatrick, D L (1958) Techniques for Evaluating Training Programmes, *Journal for the American Society of Training Directors* (now *Training and Development*), **13**

Kirkpatrick, D L (1959) Techniques for Evaluating Training Programmes, *Journal for the American Society of Training Directors* (now *Training and Development*), **14**

Kolb, D A (1984) *Experiential Learning: Experience as the source of learning and development*, Prentice Hall, New Jersey

Lee, R (1996) The Pay Forward View of Training, *People Management*, February

Legge, K (1984) *Evaluating Planned Organisational Change*, Academic Press, London

Lodge, D (1995) *Therapy*, Penguin, London

Patton, M Q (1997) *Utilisation Focused Evaluation*, 3rd edn, Sage, London

Phillips, J J (1991) *Handbook of Training Evaluation and Measurement Methods*, 2nd edn, Kogan Page, London

Stake, R E (1975) *Evaluating the Arts in Education: A responsive approach*, Charles E Merrill, Columbus

Taylor, P and Thackwray, R (1997) *Managing for Investors in People*, Kogan Page, London

Taylor, P and Thackwray, R (1999) *Investors in People Explained*, 3rd edn, Kogan Page, London

Warr, P, Bird, M and Rackham, N (1970) *Evaluation of Management Training*, Gower, London

Index